the anti-coronary cookbook

by Nathalie Havenstein and Elizabeth Richardson

GROSSET & DUNLAP

A NATIONAL GENERAL COMPANY

Publishers · New York

A Castle Books, Inc. Edition
Distributed To The Trade
By Book Sales, Inc.

Foreword

These recipes, originally published in Australia as *The Anti-Coronary Cookbook*, have been modified for United States application. In general, they conform with the suggestions of the American Heart Association for use by the "healthy" public to reduce the risk of heart attack. Many of the recipes provide useful and innovative changes for those of us who eat fat-controlled diets. Evidence now indicates that a fat-controlled diet, especially when coupled with control of high blood pressure and cessation of cigarette smoking, will be useful in reducing the occurrence of heart attack and stroke.

One word of caution: There are many people with an unusually high familial occurrence of heart attack and stroke. Members of such families often require specially designed diets for their individual problem and these diets can only be prescribed after careful clinical and laboratory examination.

CAMPBELL MOSES, M. D.
MEDICAL DIRECTOR
AMERICAN HEART ASSOCIATION

Contents

Introduction...................................... 7

Cooking Measurements and Oven Temperatures... 9

1. The Modified-Fat Diet....................... 11

2. Recipes For The Modified-Fat Diet........... 17

3. One-Week Menu For Modified-Fat Diet....... 82

4. The Calorie-Restricted Diet.................. 84

5. Recipes For Calorie-Restricted Diets.......... 93

6. One-Week Menus For Calorie-Restricted Diets..119

Index...124

Introduction

Many people find it difficult to adjust their cooking and eating habits to the general principles of weight reduction or for the reduction of cholesterol and other fats in the blood. This cookbook has been compiled to improve the diet (without sacrificing variety, palatability or satisfaction) of those persons who are overweight or who may be vulnerable to heart or arterial ailments.

Whether you have suffered a coronary heart attack, or have high blood pressure which may produce future heart disease, or simply wish to remain healthy, this cookbook can serve as a form of protection.

Whatever the state of your health, or diet plan adopted, it is essential that eating and drinking should be as pleasurable as possible, a delight and not a medicine. There are books and pamphlets available which explain, sometimes in considerable detail, the ways in which diet, blood fats (including cholesterol), obesity, coronary heart disease and other arterial diseases are possibly related. However, these texts are rarely good kitchen companions. What is needed is a comprehensive, practical book which can be the cook's constant aid, like any conventional cookbook, yet give her a wide variety of recipes which will help immensely in reducing blood fats and body weight. Hence this book.

There presently exist two "epidemics" in affluent societies that have caused diet patterns to come under scrutiny — obesity and coronary heart disease. Obesity, that is, being overweight, results from eating and drinking more calories than are expended as energy. Even a very small excess of calories each day can lead to gross obesity over a period of time. It is generally recognized that obesity is liable to cause discomfort and a variety of illnesses and that improvement can be brought about by regulating the diet, i.e., by reducing caloric intake, while still preserving a balanced diet in other respects.

The complete relation between diet and coronary heart disease, strokes and other arterial diseases is not clear. However, facts indicate that high-blood pressure, cigarette smoking and raised levels of blood fats can be associated with the development of these ailments.

The higher the concentration of cholesterol and its associated triglycerides in the blood, the greater the risk of developing disease. Today the diet to which many of us have become accustomed is high in cholesterol and saturated (animal) fat. Most of the ordinary fats in the diet are saturated fats which tend to increase the blood cholesterol. The polyunsaturated fats found in fish, nuts and most vegetables oils do not have this cholesterol elevating effect. Obviously then, a diet containing adequate but not excessive calories and a reduced content of cholesterol and saturated fat could reduce the cholesterol level and possibly retard arterial disease. In addition, because carbohydrates also affect the blood fats in some people, it would seem wise to restrict the use of refined sugars.

The effectiveness of this "modified-fats" diet awaits the results of trials by large numbers of people over a period of several years. There is already a great deal of circumstantial evidence to support the view that adherence to this form of diet would reduce the chances of developing coronary and related diseases, and many people are being advised, or are themselves deciding to try it.

Cooking Measurements and Oven Temperatures

Standard measuring cups and spoons were used for all recipes in this book. All measures are level:

1 cup	= 8 fluid ounces	These are the same size as medicinal measures or spoons used for baby foods.
1 tablespoon	= ½ fluid ounce	
3 teaspoons	= 1 tablespoon	

Flour	1 cup lightly filled	= 4 oz
Sugar, crystal	1 cup lightly filled	= 6 oz
Sugar, brown	1 cup lightly filled	= 5 oz
Sugar, granulated	1 cup lightly filled	= 6 oz
Sugar, icing	1 cup tightly filled	= 6 oz
Margarine	1 cup	= 8 oz
Polyunsaturated oil	1 cup	= 8 oz
Dried skim milk powder	1 cup	= 3 oz
Plain flour	3 tablespoons	= 1 oz
Sugar, crystal	2 tablespoons	= 1 oz
Sugar, granulated	2 tablespoons	= 1 oz
Sugar, confectioners'	2½ tablespoons	= 1 oz

Cornstarch	2½ tablespoons	= 1 oz
Gelatin	2½ tablespoons	= 1 oz
Dry crumbs	3 tablespoons	= 1 oz
Barley and Rice	2 tablespoons	= 1 oz
Currants, etc.	2 tablespoons	= 1 oz
Margarine	2 tablespoons	= 1 oz
Jam	1½ tablespoons	= 1 oz
Polyunsaturated oil	2 tablespoons	= 1 oz
Dried skim milk powder	4 tablespoons	= 1 oz

Specific oven temperatures have not been stated in any of the recipes in this book. Oven temperatures vary with the site of the elements in electric ovens. The oven used for testing these recipes was an electric oven.

For electric ovens the suggested range may be:
Hot   450–550
Moderate   350–425
Slow   275–325

For gas ovens the suggested range may be:
Hot   400–450
Moderate   325–375
Slow   250–300

□1□
The Modified-Fat Diet

The following are the general principles of the diet:

1. Restrict the consumption of egg yolks, animal fats, organ meats (e.g., liver, kidneys, brains and sweetbreads) and roe — they are high in cholesterol. Oysters, lobster, shrimp and crayfish have moderate amounts.

2. Restrict the consumption of butter, cream, whole milk, animal fats, foods containing lard, drippings, chicken fat, "hard" margarines containing coconut oil and commercially prepared cakes, cookies and pies.

These are rich in "saturated" fats which tend to raise the blood cholesterol level. "Saturated" or "hard" fats are those which usually become solid or hard when cold.

3. Substitute seed oils and "soft" or polyunsaturated margarines for some of the usual animal fat intake in your diet. Vegetable fats which remain in their "soft" or oil form when cold may be predominantly mono-unsaturated, as with olive oil, or polyunsaturated, as

with safflower oil and others mentioned later. It is the unsaturated fats which are important in this diet and to obtain maximum benefit the amount of unsaturated fat eaten each day should be at least twice the amount of saturated fat.

4. Restrict the use of sugar and refined carbohydrates, e.g. jam, honey, syrups, soft drinks, candies. In some people these foods cause a marked rise in the level of blood fats.

It is important not to increase your weight. Remember that fats supply twice as many calories as proteins and carbohydrates, so that if the fat in the diet is increased, the daily intake of either proteins or carbohydrates, or both, will have to be restricted. If overweight, then weight reduction can be combined with this Modified-Fat Diet.

POLYUNSATURATED OILS, MARGARINES AND MAYONNAISE

POLYUNSATURATED OILS

The seed oils: safflower, sunflower, soybean, corn or maize oils have a high content of polyunsaturated fats. Safflower oil has the highest content of any commonly available oil. These oils may be purchased in most supermarkets or grocery stores. Bulk purchases are usually cheaper. Peanut oil has a moderately low content of polyunsaturated fat, and olive oil contains oleic acid, a monounsaturated fat.

POLYUNSATURATED MARGARINE

Polyunsaturated margarines are those margarines which have a high content of polyunsaturated fats in the finished product. These margarines are produced by special manufacturing processes whereby a portion of the polyunsaturated nature of the fat is preserved. In many margarines the polyunsaturated fats present in the raw material are largely converted to saturated fats during the process of manufacture. Safflower oil is often used in the manufacture of the special margarines and the finished product is softer and more easily spread than ordinary margarines even when refrigerated.

POLYUNSATURATED MAYONNAISE

Most of the mayonnaises available do contain egg yolks but provide only about 8mg. of cholesterol per tablespoon.

DAILY FOOD QUANTITIES

The following is a *guide* to the quantities of foods which may be eaten each day. Foods which are high in saturated fats and cholesterol have been reduced but not entirely eliminated from the diet because this may involve unacceptably extreme changes in eating habits. The ratio of unsaturated fats to saturated fats in the diet as outlined, is greater than two to one. There may need to be a restriction in such foods as sugar, sweets, cakes and high-calorie beverages to compensate for an increased consumption of fat in the form of margarine and oil in order to avoid putting on weight.

FATS

Substitutions: The following foods have approximately the same polyunsaturated fat content:

   2 tablespoons polyunsaturated margarine
   1 tablespoon safflower oil
   2 tablespoons walnuts
1½ tablespoons polyunsaturated mayonnaise
   2 tablespoons peanut butter **+** 2 teaspoons oil
   3 tablespoons peanuts **+** 2 teaspoons oil
   (Standard measure spoons are used.)

MEATS

Chicken, veal, and fish: One or two servings each day, 3-4 oz. (cooked weight).
Lean lamb, mutton or beef: One very small serving (2 oz. cooked weight) each day. Lean pork may be eaten only occasionally. Bacon and sausages should not be eaten.

EGGS

Egg whites are unrestricted. Only one egg yolk per week or its equivalent as in cakes and desserts.

MILK

1–2 cups skim milk each day Nonfat dry skim milk powder, buttermilk or nonfat yogurt may also be used. ¼ cup cottage cheese may be substituted for ⅔ cup skim milk.

CHEESE

Cottage cheese is unrestricted because it is the only cheese which contains no butterfat. All other cheeses should be avoided.

VEGETABLES

Unrestricted.

*FRUITS AND FRUIT JUICES

Unrestricted.

*BREADS, CEREALS

Unrestricted.

*SUGARS, JAMS, SYRUPS

Restrict or omit.

*CAKES, COOKIES, PASTRY

Homemade items using unsaturated fats and oils and including no more than one egg yolk per week are permitted. It is best not to eat commercially prepared products because the exact ingredients are unknown.

*CONFECTIONERY

Sweets, etc., restrict or omit. Chocolates, fudges and caramels should be omitted.

*The above five food groups should be restricted if there is a need for weight reduction.

MISCELLANEOUS

The following may be used freely as desired — tea, coffee, low-calorie soft drinks, flavorings, herbs, spices, vinegar, pickles and relishes and beef, chicken and mushroom cubes.

ALCOHOL

Should be restricted to small amounts because it is known to raise the level of some blood fats.

WHEN DINING OUT

Select fruit juice or fruit cocktails, non-creamed soups, broiled foods (especially fish), salads, fruit or gelatin desserts. Avoid sauces and salad dressings made with butter or cream. Ask for desserts to be served without cream.

□2□
Recipes For The Modified-Fat Diet

The following recipes illustrate how unsaturated margarines and oils may be substituted for the saturated cooking fats, i.e., dripping, lard, butter or ordinary margarines.

Most of these recipes are for simple everyday dishes. A few of the more exotic dishes have been included for use on special occasions. By a few simple alterations your own favorite recipes may be adapted to suit the Modified-Fat Diet.

If this Modified-Fat Diet is to be maximally effective then *at least twice as much of the unsaturated fats as saturated fats must be eaten.* It is for this reason that the amount of unsaturated margarines or oil included in these recipes is probably more than you would normally use. To ascertain how much of the unsaturated margarine or oil each member of the family will get from a particular dish it is necessary to divide the quantity of unsaturated margarine or oil by the number of servings. This has been done for most recipes, e.g., Per serving: 2 teaspoons oil.

An egg yolk is very high in cholesterol. Because of this the number of whole eggs per recipe has been limited to one. No restriction is placed on the number of egg whites used.

SOUPS

Canned and packaged soups may be used provided skim milk, buttermilk or low fat yogurt is used as the reconstituting fluid when the directions call for milk or cream. When preparing stock from meat, cook the stock the day before it is required and chill. After removal of all fat, proceed according to the recipe.

Favorite recipes may be adapted by substituting unsaturated margarine or oil for butter, when sautéing vegetables or making the white sauce bases for soups.

Garnishes such as croutons, garlic, parsley or herb breads may be used in order to increase the amount of polyunsaturated fats eaten each day.

BASIC CREAM SOUP

2 tablespoons polyun-
saturated margarine
2 tablespoons flour
½ teaspoon salt
Pinch cayenne
pepper

1 cup skim milk
¼ cup polyunsaturated
oil
1 cup vegetable stock
(liquid in which veg-
etables were cooked)

Melt margarine in saucepan and remove from heat. Add flour, salt and pepper and stir with a wooden spoon until smooth. Stir over heat 1 minute; do not brown. Add milk all at once stirring constantly until it boils and thickens. Gradually add oil, beating well. Stir in vegetable stock until it is well blended. To this soup, add sieved or blended cooked carrots, peas, cauliflower, onions, spinach, pumpkin, tomatoes or asparagus. If preferred, vegetables may be left in small pieces. Garnish with croutons and parsley.

Garlic bread, herb bread or parsley bread (p. 79) may be served with soup.

Per serving: 5 teaspoons oil equivalent

CHILLED TOMATO SOUP

1 can condensed tomato
soup
1 cup buttermilk or 1
cup low fat yogurt
1 tablespoon lemon
juice

Few drops Tabasco
sauce
1 tablespoon finely
sliced shallots
½ cup skim milk
(optional)

Finely chopped parsley

Combine tomato soup with buttermilk or yogurt, lemon juice, sauce and shallots. Stir in skim milk. Chill. Sprinkle with parsley before serving.   Serves 4

CHINESE CHICKEN SOUP

½ cup raw chicken
strips
1 teaspoon salt
1 tablespoon cornstarch
2 tablespoons cold
water
4 cups chicken stock

2 teaspoons soy sauce
4 mushrooms, peeled
and sliced
1 tablespoon polyun-
saturated oil
1 tablespoon lemon
juice

Sprinkle chicken strips with salt and set aside. Blend cornstarch with cold water and add to stock. Add soy sauce. Bring to a boil, stirring constantly. Add chicken strips and simmer for 5 minutes. Heat oil in pan and sauté mushrooms for 5 minutes. Add mushrooms and lemon juice to soup. Simmer for 5 minutes.

Per serving: 1 teaspoon oil   Serves 4

CREOLE VEGETABLE SOUP

1 tablespoon chopped
onion
1 tablespoon polyun-
saturated oil
2 cups chicken stock
1 teaspoon mixed herbs
1 cup canned tomatoes

¼ cup cooked fresh or
frozen corn or whole
kernel canned corn
1 level tablespoon un-
cooked rice
Salt and pepper to
taste

Sauté onions in oil in large saucepan. Add all ingredients. Bring to a boil, cover and simmer for 20 minutes. Serve with croutons.

Per serving: 1 teaspoon oil   Serves 4

FISH CHOWDER

2 cups boiling water	1 cup diced raw potato
1½ teaspoons salt	Dash pepper
1 pound fish fillets	1 tablespoon chopped
6 tablespoons polyun-	parsley
saturated oil	2 cups skim milk
¼ cup chopped onion	2 tablespoons flour

Bring salted water to boil and add fish. Simmer for 15–20 minutes (do not boil). Reserve stock. Cook onions in 2 tablespoons oil until transparent. Add potatoes, pepper and fish stock. Boil 15 minutes or until potatoes are tender. Add flaked fish and parsley. Blend flour with skim milk and add to fish mixture. Allow mixture to boil, remove from heat and gradually add the remaining oil.

Per serving: 1½ tablespoons oil   Serves 4

FRENCH ONION SOUP

3 tablespoons polyun-	2 cups finely chopped
saturated oil	onion

4 cups beef stock
Salt and pepper to taste

Sauté onions in oil until golden. Add stock, seasonings and simmer ½ hour. Serve with croutons.

Per serving: 3 teaspoons oil   Serves 4

FISH

Fish contains very little saturated fat. One serving of fish contains less saturated fat than the equivalent amount of lamb, mutton, pork or beef. For this reason it is recommended that fish be included in the family menu several times a week.

Most types of fish are suitable, i.e., fresh and frozen fillets, smoked and salted fish (such as cod and kippers), canned fish (such as tuna and salmon) and fish canned in oils (such as sardines).

Do not buy fish fingers, fish cakes, etc., because you do not know how much fat or what kind of fat they contain. Commercially prepared fried fish and chips are best avoided.

The amount of polyunsaturated fat per serving can be increased by the use of polyunsaturated oils and margarines in cooking; by the addition of garnishes such as tartar sauce, parsley spread, etc.; by using fried bread crumbs as toppings and by serving side dishes of salads with polyunsaturated dressings or mayonnaises.

BAKED FISH

1½ to 2 pounds whole fish
Lemon juice
1 cup soft white bread crumbs
Salt and pepper
Sprinkle nutmeg
2 tablespoons chopped parsley
¼ cup polyunsaturated oil

Wipe the cleaned fish. Rub inside and outside of fish with lemon. Mix bread crumbs with a little salt, pepper, nutmeg, parsley and moisten with oil. Place about half mixture inside fish and secure with skewers or thread. Brush large piece of foil with oil, place fish and remaining seasoning on foil and seal securely. Bake on oiled baking sheet in moderate oven for 30 minutes.   Serves 4

Omit stuffing and season well with lemon juice, salt and pepper. Brush liberally with oil and cook as above.

Per serving: 1 tablespoon oil

BARBECUED FISH

¼ cup polyunsaturated oil

½ cup diced onion

1½ pounds fish fillets
Salt and pepper

1 cup Barbecue Sauce (p. 69)

2 tablespoons lemon juice

¼ cup water

1 tablespoon sugar

2 tablespoons Worcestershire sauce

½ teaspoon prepared mustard

Heat oil in pan, fry onion until brown then remove. Cut fillets into serving-size pieces and fry until lightly browned. Spread onion over fish, season with salt and pepper. Combine barbecue sauce with other ingredients and pour over fish. Cover and simmer until fish is cooked.

Per serving: 1 tablespoon oil   Serves 4

FISH BALLS

1 cup flaked cooked fresh or canned fish

2 cups mashed potatoes

2 tablespoons polyunsaturated oil
Salt and pepper

1 egg white
Flour or dry bread crumbs
Polyunsaturated oil for frying

Combine fish, mashed potato, oil, salt and pepper. Add egg white and beat well. Shape into balls, toss in flour or bread crumbs and fry in deep hot oil until brown.

Per serving: 2 teaspoons minimum   Makes 18 balls

FISH CASSEROLE

1 pound tomatoes
¼ cup polyunsaturated margarine
1 cup sliced onion

½ teaspoon paprika
Salt and pepper
1½ pounds fish fillets
Chopped parsley

Peel and chop tomatoes. Heat half the margarine and sauté onion until tender. Add the tomatoes and cook until well blended. Add paprika and season to taste. Cut fish fillets in 4 portions. Grease shallow casserole with remaining margarine, add fish, sauce and parsley and cover. Bake in moderate oven for 10 minutes or until cooked.

Per serving: 1 tablespoon oil   Serves 4

FISH PIE WITH HERBS

3 cups flaked cooked fish
1½ cups coating White Sauce (p. 72)
2 tablespoons polyunsaturated mayonnaise

1 tablespoon chopped parsley
Salt, pepper, grated nutmeg
1 tablespoon crushed dry tarragon

1 tablespoon chopped walnuts

Combine fish and white sauce, add mayonnaise and parsley. Season with salt, pepper, nutmeg. Arrange in ovenproof dish, top with tarragon and walnuts. Brown in moderate oven.

Per serving: 1½ tablespoons oil equivalent   Serves 4

GRILLED MARINATED FISH

1 clove garlic
½ cup polyunsaturated
oil
¼ cup white vinegar, or
dry white wine or
lemon juice

Chopped parsley
Salt and pepper
1½ pounds fish (use
whole flat fish, split
fish steaks or fillets)

Rub shallow pan or dish with garlic, mix and add oil, vinegar, chopped parsley, salt and pepper. Add fish and marinate 15 minutes, turn and marinate 15 minutes longer. Arrange fish on rack, brush with marinade and grill until done. Serve with heated marinade poured over fish.   Serves 4

GRILLED FISH WITH ITALIAN DRESSING

Substitute ½ cup Italian Dressing for above marinade.
   Per serving: 2 tablespoons oil

POACHED FISH

1½ pounds fish
1½ teaspoons salt
2 cups water
½ cup onion rings

6 peppercorns
2 bay leaves
1 tablespoon lemon
juice

1 tablespoon vinegar

Cut fish into serving pieces and rub with salt. Place fish in pan, add water, onion and seasonings. Bring to boil, cover and simmer for about 20 minutes or until fish is cooked. Serve with Horseradish Sauce (p. 73), Caper Dressing (p. 72), Tartar Sauce (p. 71) or Parsley Sauce (p. 73).   Serves 4

PSARI PLAKI

¾ cup diced onions
2 cups diced potato
1½ cups diced carrots
¾ cup diced celery
1 cup peeled, diced
tomatoes

5 tablespoons polyun-
saturated oil
1½ pounds fish fillets
Salt and pepper
Juice of ½ lemon

Dice vegetables into pieces of the same size. Heat oil in pan and fry vegetables. Place fish in greased shallow casserole, sprinkle with salt, pepper and lemon juice. Place vegetables and oil around and over fish. Cover with lid or aluminum foil and bake in moderate oven for 30 minutes or longer if necessary.

Per serving: 5 teaspoons oil   Serves 4

ROLLED FISH FILLETS AND ANCHOVY SAUCE

1½ pounds fish fillets
Lemon
Seasoned flour

Skim milk
Dried bread crumbs
Polyunsaturated oil

Wash and dry fillets and rub with lemon. Roll up and secure with wooden picks. Dredge with flour, dip in skim milk and toss in bread crumbs. Deep fry in oil until a golden brown and serve with Anchovy Sauce (p. 72).

Per serving: 1 tablespoon oil   Serves 4

SALMON WIZZ

2 cups cooked salmon
1 cup cooked peas
Fried Bread Crumbs (p. 79)

2 cups coating White
Sauce (p. 72)

Add salmon and peas to White Sauce and heat, place in casserole. Sprinkle with Fried Bread Crumbs, and place in moderate oven for 10–15 minutes.

Per serving: 5 teaspoons oil   Serves 4

SEASONED FILLETS OF FISH

½ cup soft bread
crumbs
2 tablespoons grated
onion
1 tablespoon chopped
parsley
¼ teaspoon basil

½ teaspoon salt
½ clove garlic, finely
cut
¼ cup water
1½ pounds fish fillets
¼ cup polyunsaturated
oil

Mix bread crumbs, onion, parsley, basil, salt and garlic in small bowl. Moisten these ingredients with half the water and spread over fish fillets. Roll up fillets, securing with wooden picks and place close together in shallow baking dish. Pour remainder of water into bottom of dish and brush tops of rolls with oil. Bake in moderate oven for 20–30 minutes.

Per serving: 1 tablespoon oil   Serves 4

SWEET AND SOUR TUNA

1-pound can pineapple
chunks
3 tablespoons polyun-
saturated oil
1 cup sliced celery
1 cup thinly sliced
carrots
½ cup sliced mush-
rooms, or 4-ounce
can button
mushrooms (optional)

¾ cup chopped red or
green peppers
1½ cups chicken stock
3 tablespoons vinegar
1 tablespoon soy sauce
(more if desired)
¼ cup sugar
3 tablespoons corn-
starch
½ teaspoon salt
½ teaspoon pepper

13-ounce can tuna

Drain pineapple, reserve ½ cup juice. Heat oil and sauté celery, carrots, mushrooms and peppers. Remove from pan. Add pineapple juice, vinegar, soy sauce to stock in saucepan and stir in sugar, cornstarch, salt and pepper. Bring to boil stirring constantly until mixture thickens slightly. Add cooked vegetables and tuna. Heat thoroughly, stirring occasionally.

Per serving: 3 teaspoons oil   Serves 4

VARIATIONS
Other meats or fish may be substituted for the tuna in this recipe.
Sweet and sour fish: Use fried fish pieces in batter.
Sweet and sour chicken: Use crumbed chicken pieces.
Sweet and sour veal: Use crumbed veal pieces.

MEATS

Meats are one of the major sources of animal fats in the diet and animal fats are rich in saturated fats. All visible fat must be removed from the meat prior to cooking. Even so there still remains a large amount of fat which is an integral part of the meat and is invisible.

No more than one serving of meats rich in fat such as lamb or beef should be eaten each day. Veal has very little fat and may be eaten both in larger quantities and more frequently. Pork and all pig products have a very high fat content and may be eaten only occasionally.

Always buy the lean cuts of meat. *Beef:* Buy cuts which are either lean or from which the fat is easily removed, such as rump, fillet, round and top round. Avoid cuts such as rolled roast, blade, porterhouse or T-bone steak where fat is distributed throughout the meat and cannot be removed. *Lamb:* Buy the lean cuts such as leg, loin chops and shanks. Loin chops and cutlets may be used very occasionally but all fat must be cut off before cooking. Avoid cuts such as shoulder or breast. These are usually very fatty. *Veal:* All cuts are suitable. *Pork:* All cuts of pork have a high content of fat and therefore consumption of pork must be severely restricted. Buy only the leanest cuts such as leg, loin and shoulder chops. If buying ham choose the leanest cuts, e.g., leg ham, avoiding rolled or shoulder hams. *Miscellaneous:* Do not buy bacon or sausages. Tongue and tripe may be eaten if desired.

When you have chosen your meat ask your butcher to trim away all visible fat. When you require ground meat, either ask your butcher to grind specially selected and trimmed round or top round or else do your own grinding at home. Do not buy ground meat from the butcher because you cannot be sure of its fat content.

COOKING MEAT FOR THE
MODIFIED-FAT DIET

1. Remove all visible fat when preparing meat for cooking.
2. Use only polyunsaturated margarine or oil in cooking. Brush oil or margarine over meat prior to grilling or broiling.
3. Whenever possible braises, casseroles and stews should be cooked the day before use and cooled. The fat will then rise to the top and can easily be removed.
4. When roasting meat, place it on a rack in baking dish. Always use polyunsaturated oil or margarine as

the basting agent and *not* the meat drippings which contain the saturated fats.

5. When broiling meat, always place it on a rack so that the drippings may drain away from the meat. If using an electric frypan always tilt pan so that the fat drains away from the meat.

6. If meat is marinated, the marinade may be used for basting the meat during cooking.

BEEF IN BURGUNDY

1 pound lean top round steak
2 cups sliced onion Thyme, parsley, bay leaf
5 tablespoons polyunsaturated oil
2 cups Burgundy

2 tablespoons flour
1 clove garlic, crushed
6¾-ounce can button mushrooms
1 dozen small onions or 3 large onions quartered

Trim all fat and cut meat into pieces 2½-inches square and ¼-inch thick and place in an earthenware dish. Season with salt and pepper, cover with 1 cup sliced onions, few sprigs thyme and parsley tied together, bay leaf, 2 tablespoons polyunsaturated oil and burgundy. Leave to marinate for 3 hours. Heat 3 tablespoons oil in pan, brown remaining sliced onions and remove. Add drained pieces of meat to pan, reserving liquid, and brown quickly. Add flour, cook for one minute then add strained liquid from marinade. Allow to boil and thicken. Add garlic, herbs, cover tightly and simmer gently for 2 hours. Add small onions, mushrooms and cook 30 minutes longer.

Per serving: 5 teaspoons oil   Serves 4

BRAISED STEAK

3 tablespoons polyun-
saturated oil
1 pound lean round
steak, cubed
2 cups sliced carrots
1 cup diced celery
1½ cups sliced parsnips

1½ cups sliced onions
Salt and pepper
1½ cups beef stock
¼ cup tomato sauce
1 tablespoon soy sauce
1 tablespoon Worces-
tershire sauce

Heat oil, add meat and brown well. Arrange ingredients
in a greased casserole. First the meat then vegetables and
salt and pepper. Mix stock with tomato, soy and Worcestershire sauces. Pour stock over meat and vegetables,
and bake in moderate oven 2—2½ hours.

Per serving: 3 teaspoons oil   Serves 4

BRAISED VEAL CHOPS

4 large veal chops
2 tablespoons polyun-
saturated oil
2 cups sliced onions
½ cup red pepper cut
in thin strips

1½ cups peeled and
chopped tomatoes
Salt and pepper
2 tablespoons chopped
parsley

Trim chops, remove all fat. Heat oil in pan, add chops
and onions and cook slowly for a few minutes to brown.
Add red pepper and tomatoes, season with salt and
pepper. Sprinkle on parsley. Cover, cook slowly for
approximately 25 minutes or until chops are tender.

Per serving: 2 teaspoons oil   Serves 4

MADRAS DRY CURRY

6 tablespoons polyun-
saturated oil
1 cup chopped onions
2 cloves garlic, crushed
1 tablespoon curry
powder

1 tablespoon plum jam
combined with 1 ta-
blespoon lemon juice
1 pound lean chuck
steak cut into 1-inch
cubes Salt

Heat oil, fry onion and garlic until golden. Add curry
powder, mix thoroughly then add plum jam and meat.
Cover, simmer 1½–2 hours or until meat is tender.
Add salt to taste.

Per serving: 1½ tablespoons oil   Serves 4

MALAYSIAN LAMB CURRY

1½ pounds lean lamb
chops
6 tablespoons polyun-
saturated oil
1¼ cups diced onions
2 cloves garlic

1¼ cups buttermilk
¼-½ teaspoon chili
powder
½ teaspoon turmeric
1¼ tablespoons curry
powder

Salt

Cut meat into 1-inch cubes. Place all ingredients except
salt in saucepan then add meat. Bring to boil and
simmer gently until meat is tender. Season to taste with
salt. Serve with boiled rice.

Per serving: 1½ tablespoons oil   Serves 4

MEXICAN RICE

3 tablespoons polyun-
saturated oil
½ cup uncooked rice
1 cup thinly sliced
onion
1 small clove garlic,
crushed
1 pound lean chuck
steak, ground

2 teaspoons salt
2 teaspoons chili
powder
⅓ cup tomato sauce
½ pound peeled,
roughly chopped
tomatoes
1 cup water
¾ cup raisins

Heat oil in frying pan, add rice and toss frequently until
lightly browned. Add onion, garlic and ground steak,
stirring until meat is browned. Stir in salt, chili powder,
tomato sauce, tomatoes, water and raisins. Cover,
simmer 25 minutes (stirring occasionally) or until rice
is tender.

Per serving: 3 teaspoons oil   Serves 4

ROAST SEASONED VEAL

*1 thick piece veal leg
(about 3-3½ pounds)
cut with pocket, or
boned shoulder
2 teaspoons prepared
mustard
⅔ cup finely chopped
mushrooms (optional)

¼ cup finely chopped
celery
½ cup chopped onion
2 tablespoons chopped
parsley
4 tablespoons soft
bread crumbs
Salt and pepper

6 tablespoons polyunsaturated oil

Spread prepared mustard inside pocket. Combine
mushrooms, celery, onion, parsley, bread crumbs and

*Leg of lamb may be substituted for veal leg

salt and pepper. Add 2 tablespoons oil and blend well.
Fill into pocket. Secure with skewers or string and brush
with oil. Bake in a moderate oven; allow 20–25 minutes
per pound and 25 minutes over. Baste frequently with oil.
Serve with potatoes baked in their jackets or roasted in
polyunsaturated oil.

Per serving: 1½ tablespoons oil   Serves 4

SAVORY MINCE

½ cup grated onion	½ cup chopped celery
1 pound lean beef, ground	2 tablespoons tomato sauce
¼ cup polyunsaturated oil	1 tablespoon Worcestershire sauce
¾ cup grated carrot	1 cup beef stock
½ cup grated potato	2 tablespoons flour

Salt and pepper

Fry onions and meat in oil until brown then add carrots,
potato and celery. Stir together tomato sauce, Worcestershire sauce, stock, flour and salt and pepper until well
blended and smooth. Add to meat mixture and simmer
30 minutes until cooked. This may be used as filling for
meat pies using Savory Pastry (p. 80).

Per serving: 1 tablespoon oil   Serves 4

SHREDDED VEAL AND CELERY
(Chinese Style)

1½ pounds veal steak or cutlet	Cornstarch
	Salt and pepper
1 tablespoon soy sauce	3 cups sliced celery
2 tablespoons dry sherry	6 tablespoons polyunsaturated oil
1½ cups chicken stock	1 tablespoon water

34

Cut meat into thin strips 2-inches long. Combine soy sauce, sherry and chicken stock in a bowl; add meat, cover and refrigerate overnight. Next day remove meat from marinade, drain well, reserve marinade. Add salt and pepper to cornstarch. Toss meat in this mixture. Wash celery, cut into diagonal strips ¼-inch wide. Sauté veal quickly in hot oil, remove from pan, add celery and cook quickly. Return meat to pan with marinade. Blend 1 tablespoon cornstarch with water, add to pan, stirring until sauce thickens. If too thick, add more stock.

Per serving: 3 tablespoons oil   Serves 4

SPAGHETTI WITH MEAT SAUCE

¼ cup polyunsaturated oil

½ pound finely ground lean top round

2 cloves garlic, crushed

¾ cup finely minced onion

1 pound peeled chopped tomatoes

1 teaspoon oregano or basil

1 teaspoon salt

Pepper to taste

3 tablespoons tomato paste

1 cup beef stock or dry red wine

½ pound spaghetti or macaroni

2 tablespoons polyunsaturated margarine or Garlic Spread (p. 70)

Heat oil in pan, add meat, garlic and onion. Brown lightly. Add tomatoes, oregano, salt and pepper. Blend tomato paste with beef stock and add to mixture. Simmer uncovered for 30 minutes to reduce sauce slightly. When sauce is almost ready, cook spaghetti in boiling salted water. Drain spaghetti and place on hot serving dish or plate. Fold margarine or Garlic Spread into spaghetti.

Pour hot meat sauce over spaghetti. Serve with Garlic Bread (p. 79).

Per serving: 1 tablespoon oil   Serves 4

STUFFED VEAL ROLLS

1½ pounds veal steak or cutlet
½ cup polyunsaturated oil
¾ cup finely chopped onions
2 cups soft bread crumbs
¾ cup coarsely chopped apple
Salt and pepper to taste
2 tablespoons flour
2 cups apple juice or cider
2 tablespoons cornstarch

Cut veal into serving pieces, pound with a kitchen mallet until very thin. Heat half the oil, add onions and sauté. Add bread crumbs, apple, salt and pepper and cook 4 minutes. Remove and place 2 tablespoons stuffing on each veal slice. Roll up, secure with a wooden pick, dredge with flour. Heat remaining oil and brown rolls well on both sides. Add apple juice or cider, cover and simmer 30–35 minutes or until tender. Blend cornstarch with some cold apple juice and add to gravy. Stir until it boils and thickens.

Per serving: 2 tablespoons oil   Serves 4

VEAL GOULASH

1½ pounds veal
¾ cup sliced onions
¼ cup polyunsaturated oil
1 tablespoon paprika
Salt and pepper
½ cup chicken stock
1 bay leaf
2 teaspoons lemon juice
½ cup buttermilk
1 tablespoon cornstarch

Cut veal into 2-inch cubes. Soften onion in the hot oil; add the meat and brown. Add paprika and salt and pepper to taste and cook a little longer. Add the stock, bay leaf; cover pan and simmer for 1½ hours, stirring occasionally (add more liquid if it becomes too dry). Pour lemon juice into buttermilk, blend in cornstarch and stir into veal, until thickened.

Per serving: 1 tablespoon oil   Serves 4

VEAL MARENGO

1½ pounds veal steak or cutlet
½ cup seasoned flour
Salt and pepper
¼ cup polyunsaturated oil
1 clove crushed garlic
½ cup white wine
1½ cups chicken stock
1 tablespoon tomato paste
1½ cups peeled and chopped tomatoes
1½ cups chopped onions
⅔ cup button mushrooms

Chopped parsley

Cut veal into serving pieces; dredge with seasoned flour (reserve remaining flour). Heat oil in large pan, add meat and brown. Remove and place in casserole. In same pan fry garlic a few minutes, add remaining flour and cook, stirring until lightly browned. Gradually add wine and chicken stock, bring to boil. Add tomato paste and stir. Simmer gently until reduced to half. Pour over meat. Add tomatoes, onions and mushrooms to meat, cover casserole. Bake in moderate oven until tender (approximately 1½—2 hours).

Per serving: 1 tablespoon oil   Serves 4

VEAL AND POTATO CASSEROLE

1½ pounds veal
½ cup polyunsaturated margarine
3½ cups coarsely cut onions

Salt to taste
12 whole peppercorns
2 bay leaves
4 cups diced potatoes
Chopped chives

Cut veal into cubes. Melt margarine in pan and turn meat and onions in it but do not brown. Add boiling water until the meat is just covered then add salt, peppercorns and bay leaves. Simmer for about 20 minutes. Add the potatoes, and let the mixture cook until the potatoes have blended with the meat broth giving the appearance of a very thick potato soup. Garnish with chopped chives.

Per serving: 1 tablespoon oil equivalent   Serves 4

VEAL RAGOUT

½ pound dried apricots
1½ pounds veal
½ cup polyunsaturated oil
3 cups finely chopped onions
1 clove garlic, crushed
1 cup chopped carrots
½ cup chopped turnips
Salt
1 teaspoon paprika

1 teaspoon curry powder
1 teaspoon saffron shreds
1 teaspoon cinnamon
1 teaspoon cumin
1 teaspoon whole cloves
Thyme and 2 bay leaves
Chicken stock

Soak apricots in water overnight. Cut meat into 1-inch cubes. Heat oil in a large heavy pan and brown the veal on all sides. Add the finely chopped onions and garlic and brown. Add carrots and turnips. Sprinkle salt, paprika, curry powder, saffron, cinnamon, cumin and cloves over meat and vegetables; add thyme, bay leaves, soaked apricots and apricot liquid. Pour sufficient stock over the meat and vegetables to cover. Cover and simmer gently for about 2½ hours.

Per serving: 2 tablespoons oil   Serves 4

POULTRY AND GAME

These meats have a low saturated fat content, and may be eaten frequently in relatively large quantities. The amount of polyunsaturated fats per serving can be greatly increased by the addition of such items as garlic or herb bread; salads with polyunsaturated dressings or mayonnaise; or fried vegetables. Chicken and turkey are not as fat as duck and goose.

COOKING POULTRY AND GAME
FOR THE MODIFIED-FAT DIET

1. Remove any visible fat when preparing poultry for cooking. As fat lies under the skin of chicken and turkey, prick the skin before cooking to ensure that as much of the fat as possible drains away from the bird. Do not eat the skin.

2. Use only polyunsaturated margarine or oil in cooking. Brush oil or margarine over poultry prior to broiling.

3. When roasting poultry place it on a rack in baking dish. Always use polyunsaturated oil or margarine as the basting agent *not* the drippings which contain the saturated fats.

4. If poultry is marinated the marinade may be used for basting during cooking.

CHICKEN AND ORANGE

3 oranges
Water
2½ pounds chicken
Salt and pepper
1 teaspoon paprika
¼ teaspoon ground ginger

¼ cup polyunsaturated
margarine
2 tablespoons flour
½ tablespoon brown
sugar

Peel rind from one orange, remove white pith. Cut rind into fine shreds. Juice rinded orange and one other; add water to make 1 cup. Cut chicken into serving portions, sprinkle with salt, pepper and paprika. Melt margarine in a large deep pan, add chicken and brown well. Remove chicken pieces. Stir flour into pan, add sugar and ginger. Blend well. Stir in orange juice and rind. Bring to boil, boil 2–3 minutes, adjust seasoning. Return chicken to sauce. Cover and simmer until chicken is tender. Peel third orange and divide into segments, removing membrane. Add to chicken during last 5 minutes of cooking time. Serve with plain boiled rice.

Per serving: 2 teaspoons oil   Serves 4

CHICKEN AND WALNUTS

1 ounce dried mush-
    rooms or ¼ pound
    fresh mushrooms
2-2½ cups uncooked
    chicken, diced
2 teaspoons soy sauce
2 teaspoons brandy or
    dry sherry
2 teaspoons cornstarch

¼ teaspoon salt
1 clove garlic
2 tablespoons polyun-
    saturated oil
¼ cup diced celery
1 cup chicken stock or
    water
4 ounces walnuts

Slice fresh mushrooms or soak dried mushrooms in boiling water until soft. Mix chicken with soy sauce and brandy or dry sherry and salt. Heat oil in a pan with garlic until garlic is brown. Add chicken to pan and stir briskly. When chicken is browned add celery, mushrooms and liquid. Stir well for 5–10 minutes, add walnuts. Add cornstarch, blended with 2 tablespoons cold water and boil, stirring until lightly thickened.

Per serving: 1½ tablespoons oil equivalent   Serves 4

CHICKEN IN THE BASKET

Four 1- to 1½-pound chickens or one 2- to 2½-pound chicken
Salt and pepper
Polyunsaturated margarine
2 teaspoons paprika
1 cup water or stock

Truss chicken, rub with salt and pepper. Spread breasts and thighs with margarine, place on rack in baking pan; sprinkle with paprika. Pour in stock or water. Bake in moderately hot oven 1–1¼ hours or until chickens are well browned and tender; baste frequently. Add extra water to pan during cooking if necessary. To serve, place chickens in small individual baskets lined with paper napkins.   Serves 4

CHICKEN RIOJANA

One 2- to 2½-pound chicken
Salt and pepper to taste
Seasoned flour
3 tablespoons polyunsaturated oil

Cut chicken into serving pieces, dredge with seasoned flour. Add oil to coat bottom of large pan. Fry chicken, turning for even browning. Reduce heat, cover and cook until tender, about 30–40 minutes. Serve on a bed of Rice Riojana (below) or hot boiled rice and spoon Riojana Sauce (below) over chicken pieces.

RICE RIOJANA

2 tablespoons polyun-
saturated oil
1 clove garlic, crushed
3 chopped shallots or
¼ cup chopped
onions
¼ cup chopped red
pepper
½ cup drained whole
kernel corn
1½ cups cooked long
grain rice

Heat oil. Add garlic, shallots or onion and red pepper; cook 3 minutes. Add corn and rice and toss well with fork, cooking until heated. Add salt and pepper to taste and serve sprinkled with chopped green onion.

RIOJANA SAUCE

2 tablespoons polyun-
saturated oil
¾ cup finely chopped
green onions
1 cup apricot nectar
1 tablespoon white
vinegar or 2 table-
spoons white wine
3 peeled chopped
tomatoes
1 tablespoon chopped chives

Heat oil; add onions and cook slowly until tender; do not brown. Add nectar and wine, bring to a boil and continue boiling fast to reduce liquid and thicken. Add salt and pepper to taste. Add tomatoes and chives and simmer gently to heat.

Per serving: 2 tablespoons oil   Serves 4

CREAMED CHICKEN

2-2½ pounds steamed
chicken carved into
serving pieces

3 cups coating White
Sauce (p. 72)
1 cup cooked peas

2 cups Fried Crumbs (p. 79)

Combine chicken, White Sauce and peas. Place in casserole, sprinkle with Fried Crumbs and heat in moderate oven.

Per serving: 5 tablespoons oil minimum   Serves 4

CURRIED TURKEY

6 tablespoons polyun-
saturated oil
1 cup diced onion
2 cups diced cooking
apple
Salt and pepper
2 teaspoons curry
powder

2 tablespoons flour
2 cups skim milk with 2
chicken bouillon
cubes added
1 tablespoon lemon
juice
4 cups cooked diced
turkey

Heat 4 tablespoons oil, add onion and apple and cook until tender, about 15 minutes. Remove mixture from pan, add remaining oil and carefully blend in salt, pepper, curry powder and flour. Return to heat and cook 1 minute. Remove from heat, add liquid and lemon juice and reheat, stirring constantly until mixture thickens. Add meat, apple and onion and allow to simmer for 15 minutes.

Per serving: 1½ tablespoons oil   Serves 4

HAWAIIAN RICE

6 tablespoons polyun-
saturated oil
1 cup raw rice
2 cups chicken stock
Salt and pepper to
taste
1 cup chopped onion

1 cup chopped green
or red pepper
½ cup chopped celery
1-2 teaspoons curry
powder
1-pound can pineapple
chunks

2 cups chopped cooked chicken

Heat half the oil in frying pan, add rice and brown lightly. Reduce heat, add stock and seasonings. Cover and cook gently for about 20 minutes or until rice is tender. In large saucepan heat remaining oil, add onion, pepper, celery, curry powder and cook gently until tender. Add vegetables, drained pineapple chunks and chicken pieces to rice mixture. Stir and heat thoroughly.

Per serving: 1½ tablespoons oil   Serves 4

FRIED RICE

Omit pineapple pieces, curry powder and chicken. Flavor with soy sauce.

WHOLE CHICKEN BRAISED WITH MUSHROOMS

2-2½ pounds chicken
Salt
1 cup dried mushrooms
or 6-8 fresh mushrooms
3 cloves garlic

2 teaspoons soy sauce
1 tablespoon brandy or
dry sherry
3 tablespoons polyun-
saturated oil

Salt chicken thoroughly. Scald the dried mushrooms. Crush two cloves garlic and mix well with soy sauce and brandy then rub the mixture all over the chicken. Add one clove garlic to oil and heat in a large pan until garlic browns. Place chicken in deep pan and allow to brown well; add mushrooms. Stir well, then add 2 cups water and balance of mixture (soy, brandy, etc.). Bring to boil and allow to simmer for approximately 1 hour. If required, cornstarch blended with water may be used to thicken gravy.

Per serving: 3 teaspoons oil   Serves 4

VEGETABLES

Vegetables contain no cholesterol and the small content of fat is generally unsaturated fat. There is therefore no restriction on either the variety or quantity that may be eaten. Vegetables, moreover, form good vehicles for increasing the amount of unsaturated oils and margarine which may be consumed each day. Polyunsaturated oil may be used when baking, deep or shallow frying, sautéing and mashing vegetables. Polyunsaturated margarine may be used with steamed vegetables.

GLAZED CARROTS

¼ cup chopped onion
3 tablespoons polyun-
saturated margarine
2 cups thinly sliced
carrots

⅓ cup water
Salt and pepper to
taste
½ teaspoon brown
sugar

Sauté onions in margarine until golden. Add carrots and cook a few more minutes. Add water, salt, pepper and sugar. Cover and simmer over low heat until tender.

Per serving: 1 ½ teaspoons oil equivalent   Serves 4

Substitute: peas, parsnip, sweet potato, sweet corn or red cabbage for carrots.

MASHED POTATOES

2 cups cooked potatoes	¼ cup polyunsaturated margarine or 2 tablespoons polyunsaturated oil

Mash potatoes, add margarine or oil and beat until light and fluffy.

Per serving: 2 teaspoons oil   Serves 4

SAFFRON RICE

2 cups chicken stock	¾ cup chopped onion
¼ teaspoon saffron shreds	1 clove garlic, crushed
¼ cup polyunsaturated oil	½ cup chopped green peppers
	1 cup rice

Steep the saffron in the chicken stock. Heat oil in ovenproof casserole. Add onion, garlic, peppers and rice. Turn rice until grains are well coated with oil. Add saffron-flavored chicken stock. Bring to boil, cover and bake in a moderate oven for 30 minutes.

Per serving: 1 tablespoon oil   Serves 4

SAUTEED FRENCH BEANS

1¼ cups sliced french beans	3 tablespoons water
6 tablespoons polyunsaturated margarine	Salt and pepper
	Squeeze of lemon juice
Chopped parsley	

Cook beans in margarine, water, salt, pepper and lemon juice until tender. Add parsley.

Per serving: 3 teaspoons oil equivalent   Serves 4

VARIATION
Substitute onion, carrots, marrow, tomatoes or finely shredded cabbage for french beans.

SCALLOPED POTATOES

1 pound potatoes	1 cup skim milk
Pepper and salt	2 tablespoons polyun-
1 tablespoon flour	saturated margarine

Peel potatoes and cut into ¼-inch slices. Arrange in layers in greased pie pan with a little pepper, salt and flour between each layer. Add milk and dot with margarine. Place in moderate oven for 40–45 minutes.

Per serving: 1 teaspoon oil   Serves 4

STUFFED GREEN PEPPERS

4 large green peppers	1 cup whole kernel
1 cup thick White	corn
Sauce (p. 73)	½ teaspoon mustard
1½ cups diced cold	1 cup Fried Crumbs
cooked meat	(p. 79)

Cut stem ends from peppers and remove seed. Chop ends. Place cases into boiling salted water, simmer for 5 minutes then remove. Cook chopped pepper ends for about 2 minutes in salted water, then drain. Prepare the sauce, add cold cooked meat, corn, mustard and chopped pepper ends. Fill pepper cases — they can be placed into deep muffin tins to hold them upright. Sprinkle

Fried Crumbs on top of peppers. Bake in a moderately hot oven until peppers are tender, approximately 15 minutes.

Per serving: 5½ teaspoons oil equivalent   Serves 4

TOMATO SCALLOP

1 tablespoon polyunsaturated margarine
½ cup bread crumbs
4 sliced tomatoes
2 thinly sliced cooking apples

1 cup thinly sliced onion rings
Salt and pepper
2 cups Fried Crumbs (p. 79)

Grease the bottom and sides of an ovenproof dish with margarine and sprinkle with bread crumbs. Fill the dish with layers of sliced tomato, apple and thinly sliced onion rings; season with salt and pepper. Cover with Fried Crumbs and bake at least one hour in a slow oven.

Per serving: 2 tablespoons oil   Serves 4

VEGÈTABLE SAUTE WITH TARRAGON DRESSING

2 cups beans cut into 2-inch diagonal slices
2 cups sliced zucchini
1 cup carrot slices
1 pound small white onions, sliced

2 tablespoons polyunsaturated oil
2 tablespoons polyunsaturated margarine
¼ teaspoon Tabasco sauce

Tarragon Dressing (p. 71)

Cook vegetables in boiling salted water until they are tender but still crisp; drain. Heat oil and margarine in pan. Stir in Tabasco sauce. Add all vegetables and toss gently until heated through, about 5 minutes. Serve immediately with Tarragon Dressing.

Per serving: 3 teaspoons oil minimum   Serves 4

SALADS

There are no restrictions on either the quantity or variety of vegetables which may be used for salads. Therefore the increased use of salads either as the main course or as a side dish with meat, fish or poultry is encouraged because the accompanying salad dressing can be made with oils containing polyunsaturated fats.

Polyunsaturated mayonnaise or Boiled Dressing (p. 69) may also be used as the binding agent in potato, rice, macaroni or mixed vegetable salads.

Safflower, sunflower, soybean and corn oils are recommended as the base for salad dressings because of their high content of polyunsaturated fats. Olive oil and peanut oil have a low polyunsaturated fat content and are not recommended as a base.

Cottage cheese, or Cottage Cheese Dips (p. 76), are a useful addition to salads, as a substitute for meat.

CABBAGE SALAD

2 cups finely shredded green cabbage	Salt and pepper to taste
1 tablespoon finely chopped onion	¾ cup cottage cheese Polyunsaturated mayonnaise
2 tablespoons finely chopped celery	

Combine cabbage, onion, celery, salt and pepper. Fold cottage cheese lightly through mixture. Add sufficient mayonnaise to moisten.   Serves 4

COTTAGE CHEESE POTATO SALAD

2 cups cooked diced
   potatoes
¼ cup sliced celery
1 tablespoon chopped
   green pepper
2 teaspoons chopped
   pimento
1 tablespoon grated
   onion

1 tablespoon chopped
   pickles
½ cup polyunsaturated
   mayonnaise
½ teaspoon salt
   Pinch pepper
½ teaspoon dry
   mustard
2 teaspoons lemon juice

½ cup cottage cheese

Combine potatoes, celery, green pepper, pimento, onion and pickles. Chill well. Blend mayonnaise, salt, pepper, mustard and lemon juice. Pour over potato mixture and add cottage cheese. Toss lightly.

Per serving: 3 teaspoons oil equivalent   Serves 4

ITALIAN SALAD

¾ cup cooked diced
   carrots
¾ cup asparagus cuts
¾ cup cooked peas

1 tablespoon chopped
   parsley
Polyunsaturated
   mayonnaise

Bind vegetables with mayonnaise. May also be served as an appetizer by placing on a bed of shredded lettuce in a cocktail glass.   Serves 4

MARINATED CUCUMBERS

1 peeled cucumber
   (8 ounces)

½ cup French Dressing
   (p. 70)

Slice cucumber paper thin. Cover with dressing.

Per serving: 2 tablespoons oil   Serves 4

MARINATED GREEN BEANS

1½ cups finely cut beans
2 tablespoons chopped onions
½ teaspoon coarse ground pepper

4 tablespoons vinegar
¼ cup polyunsaturated oil
Pinch of basil

Cook beans in 2 cups boiling water for 4–5 minutes. Drain well. Combine with remaining ingredients and chill.

Per serving: 1 tablespoon oil   Serves 4

RAISIN SALAD

½ cup raisins
1 cup grated carrots
¼ cup finely diced onions
¾ cup diced celery

¼ small cabbage, finely shredded
Salt and pepper
Polyunsaturated mayonnaise

Mix all ingredients together, season to taste with salt and pepper. Add sufficient mayonnaise to bind ingredients.

Serves 4

RICE SALAD

2 cups cooked rice (approximately ⅔ cup uncooked)
¼ cup polyunsaturated mayonnaise
½ cup cooked peas

½ cup diced carrots
½ cup diced red apples
1 cup finely sliced celery
2 teaspoons salt
¼ teaspoon pepper

Combine all ingredients.

Per serving: 3 teaspoons oil equivalent   Serves 4

WALDORF SALAD

2 cups diced unpeeled
red apples
2 tablespoons lemon
juice
1 cup chopped celery

½ cup polyunsaturated
mayonnaise
½ cup coarsely chopped
walnuts

Sprinkle apples with lemon juice, mix with celery, bind with mayonnaise. Chill. Just before serving add chopped walnuts.

Per serving: 2¼ tablespoons oil equivalent   Serves 4

YOGURT POTATO SALAD

2 cups yogurt
1 teaspoon caraway
seeds
1½ teaspoons curry
powder

1 tablespoon   chopped
onion
1½ teaspoons garlic salt
2 cups cold diced
potatoes

Combine yogurt, caraway seeds, curry powder, onion and garlic salt. Fold mixture into diced potatoes; chill a few hours before serving.   Serves 4

CAKES AND COOKIES

Favorite family recipes can be adapted to suit this Modified-Fat Diet by substituting skim milk for full cream milk and polyunsaturated margarine for butter or other margarines.

Egg yolks used in cakes and cookies must be counted as part of the total allowance of one per person per week. This restriction does not apply to egg whites as these do not contain cholesterol.

Commercially prepared cakes and cookies should only be used occasionally because the quantity and type of fat and the number of eggs used in their preparation are unknown. Cookies with cream fillings and those with chocolate coatings should not be eaten.

APPLE CAKE

½ cup polyunsaturated margarine
½ cup sugar
1 tablespoon chopped lemon peel

1 cup drained stewed apples
2 cups flour
1 teaspoon cinnamon
½ teaspoon allspice

Cream margarine with sugar; add lemon peel. Fold in apples, then sifted flour and spices and mix lightly but thoroughly. Pour into well-greased 8-inch round tin. Sprinkle top with Cinnamon Crumble Topping (p. 63). Bake in moderate oven for 20–25 minutes. Warm Icing (p. 60) and chopped walnuts may be used instead of Cinnamon Crumble Topping.

CHOCOLATE CAKE

½ cup polyunsaturated margarine
½ cup powdered sugar
Vanilla
2 tablespoons light corn syrup

2½ cups flour
¼ cup cocoa
4 teaspoons baking powder
1 tablespoon baking soda

1½ cups skim milk

Cream margarine with sugar, vanilla and syrup. Fold in sifted dry ingredients alternately with milk making a soft batter. Grease and line bottoms of two 8-inch cake pans with buttered paper. Divide mixture evenly. Bake in moderate oven for 30–35 minutes. Cool on cake rack, fill with Lemon Filling (below), dust top with sifted confectioners' sugar or decorate with Warm Icing (p. 60) and chopped walnuts.

LEMON FILLING

3 teaspoons cornstarch
3 tablespoons cold water
Grated rind and
juice of one lemon.

4 tablespoons sugar
1 tablespoon polyunsaturated margarine

Blend cornstarch with water. Place all ingredients in saucepan, simmer over low heat for 3 minutes, stirring constantly. Allow to cool then spread evenly between cake layers.

CHRISTMAS CAKE

3 tablespoons sherry or whisky
3 cups sultana raisins, currants and chopped raisins
⅓ cup each, glacé pineapple, apricots, cherries and dried figs
3 tablespoons glacé pears
2 tablespoons chopped orange peel
¼ cup chopped walnuts
2 cups water

1¾ cups sugar
¼ cup light corn syrup
½ cup polyunsaturated margarine
4 cups flour
1 teaspoon baking soda
1 teaspoon each, cinnamon and nutmeg
¼ teaspoon salt
1 teaspoon each, vanilla and lemon essence
3 drops almond essence

Combine fruits, peel and walnuts and soak in sherry overnight. Place water, sugar, syrup, margarine and fruit into a saucepan and bring to boil. Boil for 10 minutes, cool. Add sifted dry ingredients and vanilla, lemon and almond essence. Pour into a well-lined 8-inch round or square pan and bake in very moderate oven for 1¼–1½ hours.

FRUIT NUT LOAF

½ cup sultana raisins
1 cup water
¼ cup sugar
¼ cup polyunsaturated margarine

1 teaspoon baking soda
1 egg
1 teaspoon cinnamon
½ cup chopped walnuts
2 cups flour

Pinch salt

Place raisins, water, sugar, margarine and soda into a saucepan, bring to a boil, simmer three minutes, then allow to cool. Add beaten egg, cinnamon and walnuts. Fold in sifted flour and salt. Pour into greased loaf pan and bake in moderate oven 35–40 minutes. Serve cold, cut into slices and spread with polyunsaturated margarine.

GINGERBREAD

1 teaspoon baking soda
1 cup skim milk
2 teaspoons ground ginger
1 teaspoon cinnamon
1 teaspoon mixed spice
2 cups flour

½ cup polyunsaturated margarine
¼ cup powdered sugar
1 cup warm light corn syrup
¼ cup walnuts
1 cup mixed fruit, including peel

Dissolve the soda in the milk. Add spices to sifted flour. Cream margarine and sugar thoroughly and beat in the corn syrup. Fold milk and flour alternately into creamed mixture. Add walnuts and mixed fruit. Bake in 8-inch square baking pan in slow to moderate oven, approximately 30 minutes. Ice with lemon icing when cold and decorate with pieces of candied ginger or lemon peel, or spread slices with polyunsaturated margarine.

ORANGE AND RAISIN SLICE

½ cup polyunsaturated margarine
1 cup brown sugar
1 egg
1 cup sifted flour
½ teaspoon soda
1 teaspoon baking powder
¼ teaspoon salt
1 cup buttermilk
1 cup raisins
Rind and juice of 1 small orange
1 cup rolled oats

Cream margarine; gradually add sugar, creaming thoroughly. Add egg and beat until light and fluffy. Sift together flour, soda, baking powder and salt. Add to creamed mixture alternately with buttermilk. Chop raisins finely, mix with orange juice and rind. Fold mixture into batter. Add rolled oats, mix lightly until combined. Bake in a greased 7 × 11-inch loaf pan in a moderate oven for 45 to 50 minutes.

May be served as a hot dessert with Hard Sauce (p. 65) or Custard (p. 64).

ORANGE BISCUITS

⅔ cup brown sugar
4 tablespoons polyunsaturated oil
1 egg white
¼ cup orange juice
1 teaspoon grated orange rind
1½ cups sifted flour
½ teaspoon soda
½ teaspoon baking powder
Chopped walnuts

Mix brown sugar with oil, beat in egg white, add orange juice and half of orange rind. Sift flour with soda and baking powder and stir into mixture. Drop by teaspoonful on to baking sheet and bake about 8–10 minutes in moderate oven. When biscuits are cool, ice with Orange Icing (p. 60) and decorate with walnuts.

PLAIN SCONES

2 cups flour
1 tablespoon
  confectioners' sugar

2 tablespoons polyun-
  saturated margarine
About ¾ cup skim
  milk

Combine sifted flour with sugar. Melt margarine, add to milk. Pour liquid all at once into dry ingredients. Mix quickly into soft dough. Turn onto floured board and knead lightly and quickly. Roll out to ½- to ¾-inch thick and cut into desired shape. Place on lightly greased baking sheet. Glaze with milk. Bake in hot oven for 10–12 minutes.

VARIATIONS
Add to above mixture:
Spicy fruit scones: 1 teaspoon mixed spices, ¼ cup chopped mixed fruit.
Raisin scones: ½ cup chopped sultana raisins.
Date scones: ¼ cup chopped dates.
Currant scones: ¼ cup currants.
Walnut scones: ¼ cup chopped walnuts.
Orange scones: grated rind and juice of one orange. Reduce quantities of milk so that total liquid used equals ¾ cup. Brush with orange juice and sprinkle with sugar before baking.

WALNUT CRESCENTS

Pastry:

½ cup cottage cheese
1 cup flour

½ cup polyunsaturated
margarine

Mix ingredients and knead thoroughly. Cover and let stand 2–12 hours. Roll pastry thinly, cut and fill. Bake in moderately hot oven.

Walnut Filling:

1 cup walnut pieces
6 tablespoons sugar

⅓ cup hot skim milk

The following are optional but improve the flavor:

Grated lemon peel
Cinnamon
1 tablespoon honey
2 tablespoons sultana raisins

Grind walnuts finely, pour boiling milk over them. Add rest of ingredients. Roll pastry out thinly. Cut into squares about 3 × 3 inches. Place walnut mixture in center, fold a corner of a square in about halfway so that folded corner will cover the filling, then roll the triangle and bend it in the shape of a crescent. Bake in moderately hot oven. When cool dust with confectioners' sugar.

VARIATIONS
Jam Triangles
Roll out pastry, cut into 2 × 2-or 3 × 3-inch squares, add jam. Fold in half diagonally, pressing down edges. Bake as above. When cool dust with confectioners' sugar.

Apple Strudel

Filling:

1 cup hot Fried
Crumbs (p. 79)

4 coarsely grated or
thinly sliced large
apples

3 tablespoons sultana
raisins

3 tablespoons sugar

1 teaspoon cinnamon
Grated rind of 1
lemon

Pinch powdered cloves

Roll out pastry into large rectangle. Fill center with apple, sprinkle with remaining ingredients. Leave outer edges of pastry free of filling. Fold pastry in from the sides to overlap in the center and slightly fold in the ends so that filling is completely enclosed. Bake as above. When cool dust with confectioners' sugar.

MOCK CREAM

3 tablespoons polyun-
saturated margarine

2 tablespoons sugar

1 tablespoon boiling
water

1 tablespoon cold skim
milk

Vanilla

Beat margarine and sugar until light and fluffy. Gradually add boiling water then milk, beating well. Flavor with vanilla. Use with desserts and as fillings for cakes, biscuits, etc.

VIENNA MOCK CREAM

2 tablespoons polyun-
saturated margarine

1 teaspoon vanilla essence

8 tablespoons sifted
confectioners' sugar

1 tablespoon skim milk

Combine all ingredients. Whip until light and fluffy. Use as a filling or force through an icing tube to decorate cakes or tarts, colored and flavored as desired.

WARM ICING

1 cup confectioners' sugar

1 tablespoon polyunsaturated margarine (melted)

Water

Sift sugar and mix with melted margarine and a little water until icing is smooth and thick. Warm slightly over low heat. Use as required.

VARIATIONS
Coffee: Add 1 teaspoon instant coffee powder to confectioners' sugar.
Chocolate: Add 1 tablespoon cocoa to confectioners' sugar.
Lemon: Use strained lemon juice instead of water.
Orange: Use strained orange juice instead of water.

DESSERTS

Favorite recipes can be adapted to meet this Modified-Fat Diet by substituting skim milk for full cream milk, and polyunsaturated margarine for butter or other margarines. Commercially prepared ice creams and milk ices contain saturated fats and these products must be eaten only occasionally. Desserts which do not require egg yolk, butter, cream or full cream milk are unrestricted. Use polyunsaturated margarine or oil for greasing tins, ovenproof dishes and paper in preparing desserts.

BAKED APPLE ROLL

1 cup flour
1 teaspoon cinnamon
5 tablespoons polyun-
    saturated margarine
3 tablespoons water

1½ cups cooked apples
    (sweetened to taste)
½ cup sultana raisins
½ cup chopped walnuts
¼ cup brown sugar

½ cup boiling water

Sift flour and cinnamon into bowl. Rub in 4 tablespoons margarine until mixture resembles bread crumbs. Mix with water to firm dough. Turn on to floured board and roll to an oblong shape ¼-inch thick. Mix cooked apples, raisins and walnuts. Cover the roll with apple mixture leaving 1-inch margin all around. Roll up, close ends and place in pie pan. Dissolve brown sugar and 1 tablespoon margarine in boiling water and pour this around the roll. Bake in hot oven 20 minutes, reduce to moderate and bake 30–35 minutes. Serve warm with Custard (p. 64).

Per serving: 4 teaspoons oil   Serves 4

BANANA FLAMBE

4 bananas
    Lemon juice
½ cup sugar
1 teaspoon cinnamon

Polyunsaturated
margarine
6 tablespoons warmed
brandy

Peel and halve bananas, place in shallow ovenproof dish and sprinkle with lemon juice. Combine sugar and cinnamon and sprinkle over bananas. Dot liberally with margarine. Place under medium hot grill until soft and golden. Take to table, pour brandy over and ignite.

Serves 4

CHOCOLATE SAUCE PUDDING

1 cup flour
1 tablespoon cocoa
¾ cup sugar
6 tablespoons polyun-
saturated margarine

½ cup skim milk
1 teaspoon vanilla
2 cups hot water
¾ cup brown sugar
1 tablespoon cocoa

Sift together flour and cocoa, add sugar. Heat margarine and milk in saucepan, add vanilla. Add to flour mixture and beat until smooth. Pour into greased deep oven-proof dish. Combine remaining ingredients and sprinkle over pudding. Gently pour hot water over. Bake in moderate oven for 40–45 minutes. (1 tablespoon of chopped walnuts may be added to the batter).

Per serving: 3 teaspoons oil equivalent   Serves 4

CHEESE CAKE

1 cup flour
4 tablespoons con-
fectioners' sugar

6 tablespoons polyun-
saturated margarine
2 tablespoons skim milk

Sift flour and sugar into bowl. Rub in margarine. Add skim milk and mix until mixture forms a ball. Spread over base of greased spring form. Bake in a moderate oven for 10–15 minutes.

Filling:

2 teaspoons gelatin
Pinch salt
1 egg
½ cup skim milk
Rind and juice 1
large lemon

1½ cups cottage cheese
¼ cup dried skim milk
powder
Vanilla
6 tablespoons sugar

Mix together gelatin and salt. Separate egg, beat yolk with skim milk. Add gelatin mixture, stir over low heat until gelatin dissolves. Remove from heat, add lemon rind, cool. Sieve cheese, beat in dried skim milk powder, gelatin mixture, lemon juice, vanilla and 4 tablespoons sugar. Beat egg white until stiff, gradually add remainder of sugar and beat well. Fold into cheese mixture. Spoon onto prepared base and refrigerate until firm.

Per serving: 1 teaspoon oil equivalent   Serves 12

CINNAMON CRUMBLE TOPPING

¼ cup brown sugar
½ cup melted polyun-
    saturated margarine

¾ cup flour
¾ cup crushed corn-
    flake crumbs

2 teaspoons cinnamon

Cream sugar and melted margarine and mix in other ingredients. Sprinkle over top of cakes or stewed fruit before placing in the oven.

CHRISTMAS PUDDING

9 tablespoons polyun-
    saturated margarine
1½ cups flour
3 cups soft white bread
    crumbs
1½ cups brown sugar
1½ cups chopped sultana
    raisins
1½ cups chopped raisins
¾ cup currants

⅓ cup chopped orange
    peel
½ cup chopped walnuts
⅓ cup grated carrots
1 tablespoon baking
    soda
1½ cups skim milk (or 1
    cup skim milk + ½
    cup brandy)
Vanilla extract

Rub margarine into flour, add bread crumbs, brown sugar and prepared fruits, nuts and carrots. Dissolve soda in milk and add to dry ingredients, add flavoring.

Grease a 3-quart pudding mold and fill it ¾ full. Tie muslin pudding cloth over top securely and place into saucepan of boiling water. Steam 3 hours. Store in cool dry place. If storing in deep freeze turn onto a plate and wrap in foil. When required steam 2 hours.

Serves 12

CREAMED RICE

¼ cup polyunsaturated margarine	½ cup water
	2 cups skim milk
3 tablespoons rice	2 tablespoons sugar

Grease ovenproof dish with a little margarine. Put rice and water in dish and cook in slow oven until rice absorbs water, stirring occasionally. Melt 2 tablespoons margarine gently and whisk into skim milk and sugar. Add to rice, sprinkle with nutmeg and bake in a slow oven for 1–1½ hours.

Per serving: 2 teaspoons oil equivalent   Serves 4

CUSTARD

2 tablespoons custard powder	2 tablespoons sugar
	½ cup polyunsaturated oil
1 pint skim milk	

Vanilla

Blend custard powder with a little milk until smooth and free from lumps. Place remaining milk and sugar into saucepan and heat until not quite boiling. Remove from heat, stir in blended custard powder and return to heat. Stir continuously until mixture boils and thickens; add vanilla. Remove from heat and beat in the oil gradually.

Per serving: 2 tablespoons oil   Serves 4

HARD SAUCE

½ cup polyunsaturated margarine
1 cup confectioners' sugar
⅓ cup brandy or sherry

Cream margarine and sugar until light and fluffy. Gradually beat in brandy or sherry.

ICE CREAM

2 cups water
1 cup dried skim milk powder
3 tablespoons sugar
2 teaspoons gelatin dissolved in 2 tablespoons boiling water
¼ cup polyunsaturated margarine
Flavorings (see below)

To warm water, add powdered milk and sugar and beat well. Add the dissolved gelatin, melted margarine and beat for 5 minutes. Turn refrigerator to maximum. Quick freezing makes a smoother ice cream. Pour mixture into refrigerator trays and chill. When ice cream is firm but not hard (approximately ¾ hour) remove from trays and beat until double its volume. Do this as quickly as possible. Add flavoring. Pour into two trays, return to refrigerator and when firm turn control to normal setting.

FLAVORINGS:
Vanilla Ice Cream: 2 teaspoons vanilla.
Orange Ice Cream: 2 teaspoons grated orange rind.
Coffee Ice Cream: 1 tablespoon instant coffee powder blended with a little hot water and added to mixture.
Chocolate Ice Cream: 6 tablespoons cocoa blended with a little hot water and added to mixture.

Strawberry Ice Cream: ½ cup crushed strawberries.
Banana Ice Cream: ¾ cup mashed bananas sprinkled with lemon juice.
Pineapple Ice Cream: ¾ cup drained crushed pineapple substituting 2 tablespoons pineapple syrup for water.
Mocha and Walnut Ice Cream: 2 teaspoons instant coffee powder and ¼ cup cocoa blended with a little hot water and ¼ cup chopped walnuts.

JUNKET

1½ tablespoons sugar
2 cups skim milk
2 junket tablets

2 teaspoons vanilla essence

Add sugar to milk and heat to lukewarm. Crush junket tablets and dissolve in a little water. Add crushed junket tablets and vanilla to skim milk and pour into dish, sprinkle with nutmeg. Stand aside to set.

VARIATIONS
Coffee: Add 1 tablespoon powdered instant coffee to skim milk.
Colored: Few drops of coloring.
Chocolate: Mix 1 level tablespoon cocoa and 1 tablespoon boiling water and add to milk.

LEMON MERINGUE PIE

1 recipe Sweet Pastry (p. 68)
6 tablespoons sugar
½ cup lemon juice
Grated rind 1 lemon
1 cup water

5½ tablespoons cornstarch
½ cup polyunsaturated margarine
2 egg whites
4 tablespoons sugar

Roll pastry out to fit 8- or 9-inch pie pan, prick well and bake in moderate oven for 10–15 minutes. Combine sugar, lemon juice, lemon rind, water and cornstarch and blend well. Boil for three minutes, stirring continually. Add margarine and beat well. Allow to cool then pour into cooked pie shell. Beat egg whites until stiff, gradually add sugar and beat well. Spoon on top of lemon filling. Return pie to oven until meringue has browned.

Per serving: 1½ tablespoons oil   Serves 6

PANCAKES

1 cup flour
  Pinch salt
2 cups skim milk
2 egg whites

1 tablespoon polyun-
  saturated oil
Polyunsaturated
  margarine

Sift flour and salt into a bowl. Make a well in center, add milk, gradually stirring into the flour. When all milk is added the mixture should be smooth and thin. Beat egg whites until just stiff and fold evenly into the batter. Stir in the oil. Pour mixture into a jug. Heat a little margarine in frying pan until well browned. Wipe pan and melt a little more margarine. When this is just bubbling, pour in sufficient batter to make thin pancakes the size you desire. Pancakes may be used as dessert or as a savory dish when filled with meat or fish filling.

Makes 9–12 pancakes

QUICK BANANA DESSERT

4 bananas
  Lemon juice
6 tablespoons orange
  juice
½ cup sugar

1 teaspoon cinnamon
¼ cup chopped walnuts
Polyunsaturated
  margarine

Peel and halve bananas, place in a shallow ovenproof dish and sprinkle with lemon juice. Pour in orange juice. Combine sugar, cinnamon and walnuts and sprinkle over bananas. Dot liberally with margarine, place in moderate oven and bake until soft and golden.   Serves 4

SWEET PASTRY

2 cups plain flour	10 tablespoons polyun-
½ teaspoon salt	saturated margarine
2 tablespoons con-	¼ cup iced water
fectioners' sugar	

Sift flour, salt and sugar into a bowl and rub in the polyunsaturated margarine until mixture resembles fine bread crumbs. Add small amounts of iced water and mix into pastry dough with a knife. Divide dough in half and roll out each piece on a lightly floured board. Sufficient pastry for two 8-inch pie shells or one double-crust pie.

SAUCES AND DRESSINGS

Sauces, spreads, dressings and mayonnaises, besides adding to the appearance and flavor of foods, are also an excellent method of including extra polyunsaturated fats.

Use white sauces for: basis of creamed soups; garnish for vegetables, fish, poultry and meat; basis of fish cakes, etc.

Use spreads for: making savory breads; garnishes for cooked vegetables; spread bread or toast used as bases for appetizers.

Use dressings for: raw salad greens, coleslaw, sliced tomato and cucumber; cooked string beans, asparagus, broccoli; marinating and basting meat, fish and poultry.

Use mayonnaises for: potato, rice or macaroni salads; on cooked vegetables such as broccoli, asparagus and cauliflower; on poached or fried fish; in salmon or tuna salads; salad of cooked chicken or veal with vegetables; on raw salad greens.

BARBECUE SAUCE

½ cup finely chopped onion
2 tablespoons brown sugar
1 teaspoon salt
1 teaspoon mustard
Pinch cayenne pepper

1 tablespoon Worcestershire sauce
¼ cup vinegar
½ cup tomato sauce
1 cup water
¼ cup mustard pickle

Combine all ingredients in a saucepan and stir until well mixed. Simmer for 15 minutes. Serve hot with barbecue meats, sausages, meat loaves or fish.

Makes 1¼ cups

BOILED SALAD DRESSING

2 tablespoons polyunsaturated margarine
½ cup flour
2 cups skim milk
½ cup polyunsaturated oil

1 teaspoon salt
Pepper
½ cup vinegar (tarragon preferably)
1½ tablespoons French mustard

Melt margarine in saucepan, add half the flour and blend well. Blend remainder of flour with milk until smooth. Take from heat and add liquid all at once, stirring constantly. Return to heat and stir until mixture boils and thickens. Remove from heat and gradually beat in the oil, then fold in salt, pepper, vinegar and mustard. Bottle and keep in refrigerator. May need diluting with skim milk before use.

Per 1 cup: 3 tablespoons oil

Makes approximately 3 cups

FRENCH DRESSING

¼ cup polyunsaturated oil
1 tablespoon vinegar
Salt, freshly ground pepper to taste

1 teaspoon sugar
½ teaspoon French mustard
1 small clove garlic, crushed

Place all ingredients in screwtop jar and shake thoroughly until blended. Store in refrigerator. Shake well before using.

Per serving: 1 tablespoon oil   Serves 4

GARLIC SPREAD

½ cup polyunsaturated margarine

2 cloves garlic, crushed
Pepper and salt

Cream margarine, garlic and seasoning until well blended. Store in refrigerator in airtight container.

VARIATIONS

Parsley spread: Omit garlic. Add 1 tablespoon chopped parsley.

Herb spread: Omit garlic. Add 1–2 teaspoons dried mixed herbs or 1 tablespoon finely chopped chives, tarragon, thyme, etc.

PIQUANT SAUCE

2 tablespoons tomato
sauce
2 tablespoons Wor-
cestershire sauce

1 tablespoon vinegar
2 tablespoons polyun-
saturated oil
2 teaspoons sugar

Place all ingredients in screwtop jar and shake thoroughly until blended. Store in refrigerator. Shake before
using.

Per 2 tablespoons sauce: 1 teaspoon oil

TARTAR SAUCE

1 cup polyunsaturated
mayonnaise or Boiled
Dressing (p. 69)
1 tablespoon chopped
gherkin
Juice of ½ lemon

¼ teaspoon finely
chopped herbs
1 teaspoon chopped
capers
1 teaspoon white or
tarragon vinegar

1 tablespoon chopped parsley

Stir all ingredients into mayonnaise. Can be stored in
refrigerator in screwtop jar.

Per 1 cup: 3 tablespoons oil

TARRAGON DRESSING

½ cup polyunsaturated
margarine
1 teaspoon tarragon
vinegar
1 teaspoon lemon juice
¼ teaspoon Tabasco
sauce

2 tablespoons polyun-
saturated mayonnaise
Salt and freshly
ground pepper to
taste

Blend all ingredients and season to taste. Spoon into
serving bowl, cover and chill until needed.

Per 2 tablespoons dressing: 1 tablespoon oil equivalent

WHITE SAUCES

Pouring sauce: Use as a foundation for soup

1 tablespoon polyun- saturated margarine	¼ cup polyunsaturated oil
1 tablespoon flour	Salt and pepper to taste
½ pint skim milk	

Melt margarine in saucepan but do not allow to boil. Remove from heat, add flour, salt and pepper and stir until smooth. Stir over heat for 1 minute but do not allow it to brown. Remove from heat. Add skim milk at once then set over heat and stir continually until sauce boils and thickens. Turn off heat and continue cooking for 2–3 minutes. Gradually add polyunsaturated oil, beating well after each addition. Season with salt and pepper.

Per 1 cup sauce: 4½ tablespoons oil

Coating Sauce: Use with vegetables as sauces and in scalloped dishes

2 tablespoons polyun- saturated margarine	¼ cup polyunsaturated oil
2 tablespoons flour	Salt and pepper to taste
1 cup skim milk	

Prepare as for Pouring sauce

Per 1 cup sauce: 5 tablespoons oil

VARIATIONS

Add to every cup of sauce:

Anchovy Sauce: 1 tablespoon anchovy essence or ½ can mashed anchovy fillets.

Caper Sauce: 1 tablespoon chopped caper and few drops vinegar.

Parsley Sauce: 1 tablespoon finely chopped parsley.
Boiled Onion Sauce: ½ cup chopped boiled onion.
Tomato Cream Sauce: 2 tablespoons tomato paste.
Horseradish Sauce: 1 tablespoon horseradish relish.
Sweet White Sauce: 1 tablespoon sugar and vanilla to flavor.

Thick Sauce: Use as foundation for savory fillings

3 tablespoons polyunsaturated margarine	¼ cup polyunsaturated oil
3 tablespoons flour	Salt and pepper to taste
½ pint skim milk	

Prepare as for Pouring sauce
Per 1 cup sauce: 5½ tablespoons oil

Panada Sauce: Use as foundations for croquettes, fish cakes, etc.

4 tablespoons flour	¼ cup polyunsaturated oil
1 cup skim milk	
Salt and pepper to taste	

Blend flour with skim milk. Bring slowly to boil, stirring constantly. Cook for a few minutes. Season with salt and pepper.
Per 1 cup sauce: ¼ cup oil

BEVERAGES

Because saturated fats must be reduced, all forms of full cream milk must be avoided whether in the form of homogenized, pasteurized, evaporated, condensed or dried full cream milk. Cream must not be used in coffee.

The use of skim milk (i.e., milk from which the cream has been removed) is unrestricted. Buttermilk and low-fat yogurt may be substituted for skim milk.

BUTTERMILK PUNCH

3 cups chilled butter-
milk
¾ cup orange juice
½ teaspoon nutmeg

1½ tablespoons lemon
juice
1½ tablespoons sugar
½ teaspoon cinnamon

Combine ingredients, beat until blended. Pour into chilled glasses. Garnish each with a thin orange slice and a sprig of fresh mint.   Serves 4

CHOCOLATE MILK SHAKE

1 cup Filled Milk
(below)
2 teaspoons chocolate
flavor

Sugar, if desired
Polyunsaturated Ice
Cream, if desired
(p. 65)

Mix all ingredients together in blender or with egg beater.

VARIATIONS
Banana: Add ½ banana and nutmeg to taste

FILLED MILK

2 cups skim milk

¼ cup polyunsaturated
oil

Pour skim milk into screwtop bottle or covered jug. Add oil. Store in refrigerator. Shake well before using. May be used with cereals at breakfast or as plain milk drink. When used in tea or coffee oil drops form on top of the beverage.

Per ½ pint milk: 2 tablespoons oil

ICED COFFEE

⅔ cup cold strong black coffee

⅔ cup cold skim milk

1-3 tablespoons poly-unsaturated oil

4 tablespoons Polyun-saturated Ice Cream (p. 65)

1 teaspoon sugar

¼ teaspoon vanilla

Cinnamon

Mix all ingredients together in blender until thick and foamy. Add extra ice cream, sprinkle with cinnamon and serve.

MOCHA CREAM

2 teaspoons cocoa

2 teaspoons sugar

1 cup cold skim milk

2 tablespoons cold strong black coffee or 2 teaspoons instant coffee powder

1-3 tablespoons poly-unsaturated oil

4 tablespoons Polyun-saturated Ice Cream (p. 65)

¼ teaspoon vanilla

Blend cocoa and sugar with a little skim milk. Stir in remaining skim milk. Mix all ingredients in blender or with egg whisk until thick and foamy. Add extra ice cream and serve.

MISCELLANEOUS

PARTY BREAD CASES

1 loaf fresh sliced bread

½ cup melted polyun-saturated margarine

Remove crusts from bread and brush both sides of bread lightly with melted margarine and press into deep patty tins. Bake in moderate oven for 15 minutes until golden brown. Fill with: Sweet and Sour Tuna, Devilled Chicken, etc.

CROUTONS

1 loaf sliced bread   **Polyunsaturated oil**

Cut bread slices into cubes, squares, triangles, circles or fancy shapes. Deep fry in oil until golden brown. Drain. May be used as garnish for soups, creamed dishes and as bases for savories.

COTTAGE CHEESE DIPS

1 cup cottage cheese   **2 teaspoons skim milk**
3 tablespoons polyun-
saturated margarine

Beat cheese and margarine until light and very smooth, then beat in skim milk. Add selected flavoring. Chill 1 hour before use.

VARIATIONS
Add to above recipe:
Chive and cucumber: 1 tablespoon chopped and well drained cucumber, 1 teaspoon salt, pinch cayenne pepper, chopped chives.
Horseradish: ¼ teaspoon salt, 2 teaspoons bottled or fresh horseradish, pinch cayenne.
French onion: 3 tablespoons French onion soup.
Herb: 1 clove garlic, crushed, 2 teaspoons grated onion, ¼ teaspoon salt, pinch mustard, ¼ cup mayonnaise, ¼ teaspoon thyme, dash Tabasco sauce. Omit skim milk.

Caraway and capers: 2 teaspoons capers, 1 tablespoon caraway seeds, 1 teaspoon finely grated onion.

Celery: 2 teaspoons finely grated onion, 1 teaspoon Worcestershire sauce, 2 tablespoons chopped celery, salt and pepper.

Gherkin: Dash paprika, 2 gherkins chopped, 1 tablespoon onion, salt and pepper.

Pineapple savory: 2 tablespoons crushed pineapple, well drained, 2 tablespoons finely chopped walnuts.

Curried salmon: 1 teaspoon curry powder, salt, pepper, 4 tablespoons salmon, 1 tablespoon finely chopped onions.

COTTAGE CHEESE NUT BALLS

1 cup cottage cheese	Cayenne pepper
1 tablespoon chopped gherkins	Chopped walnuts

Combine cottage cheese and chopped gherkins and season with cayenne pepper. Roll into balls and toss in chopped nuts. Chill at least one hour before serving.

DEVILLED WALNUTS

4 tablespoons chopped walnuts	3 tablespoons chopped parsley
3 tablespoons polyun-saturated margarine	2 tablespoons chutney Salt and cayenne
6 tablespoons cottage cheese	pepper Chili strips

Party Bread Cases (p. 75)

Sauté walnuts in margarine. Mix in cheese, parsley, chutney, salt and cayenne. Fill Bread Cases. Reheat before serving and garnish with chili strips.

FILLINGS FOR ROLLS AND SANDWICHES

Chicken and Celery: Equal parts of minced chicken and celery, seasoned with salt and moistened with a little polyunsaturated mayonnaise or Boiled Dressing (p. 69). Fish may be substituted for the chicken.

Peanut Butter and Onion: Beat together 1 cup peanut butter and ¼ cup polyunsaturated mayonnaise or Boiled Dressing (p. 69) and 1 tablespoon finely chopped onion.

Salmon and Cucumber: Flake the salmon, blend with polyunsaturated mayonnaise -or Boiled Dressing (p. 69). Add minced cucumber and mix. Season with a little salt and lemon juice. Tuna may replace the salmon.

Cottage Cheese and Gherkins: Blend polyunsaturated margarine into cottage cheese until it is a creamy consistency. Add chopped gherkins. Any combination of the following, may replace gherkins: chopped celery, walnuts, tomato, cucumber, onion, chicken, rabbit or fish.

Walnuts, Raisins and Orange: Mix 2 tablespoons chopped raisins, 2 tablespoons chopped walnuts and grated rind of one orange. Moisten with polyunsaturated mayonnaise.

FRITTER BATTER

1 cup flour	½ cup tepid water
Pinch salt	(2 parts cold, 1 part
1 tablespoon polyun-	boiling)
saturated oil	White of 1 egg

Sift flour and salt into basin. Make a well in center. Pour in oil. Stir in flour gradually with the back of a wooden spoon and add water, a little at a time, beating to a smooth batter. Beat egg white stiff and fold it in very lightly just before using. This batter is used to coat pineapple, fish pieces, banana, apple, corn, meat pieces, chicken pieces, etc.

GARLIC BREAD

1 loaf French bread   Garlic Spread (p. 70)

Slice diagonally through top to within ½ inch of loaf base. Spread Garlic Spread thickly between slices. Wrap loaf in foil and place in moderate oven for about 15–20 minutes.

VARIATIONS

Herb Bread: Use Herb Spread (p. 70).
Parsley Bread: Use Parsley Spread (p. 70).

FRIED CRUMBS

**6 tablespoons polyun-   2 cups soft white bread
saturated oil   crumbs**

Heat oil, add bread crumbs, tossing continually until golden brown. Drain on absorbent paper. Store in airtight container. Makes approximately 1½ cups.

LENTEN VEGETABLE PIE

**2 cups sliced tomatoes   5 tablespoons polyun-
1 cup onion rings   saturated margarine
1½ cups cooked macaroni   Salt and pepper
1 cup cottage cheese   1 cup mashed pumpkin
1 teaspoon mixed dried   1 cup flour
herbs (optional)   Skim milk if required
2 teaspoons chopped
parsley**

Place layers of tomato, onion, macaroni, cottage cheese, herbs and parsley into an 8-inch pie pan. Pour 4 tablespoons melted margarine over vegetables and season to taste. Place in a moderate oven and bake until vegetables are cooked. Mash pumpkin, add 1 tablespoon margarine and flour and mix to a stiff dough using skim milk if required. Roll out on a floured board to fit an 8-inch pie pan and place on filling. Brush with milk and bake in a hot oven for 15–20 minutes.

Per serving: 2 teaspoons oil equivalent   Serves 4

PIZZA PIE

1 pound fresh tomatoes	2 cups flour
9 tablespoons polyun-saturated oil	½ teaspoon salt
	⅔ cups skim milk
1 clove garlic, crushed	1 can anchovy fillets
Salt and pepper to taste	6 sliced stuffed olives
	½ cup cottage cheese

Peel and chop tomatoes. Place in pan with ¼ cup oil and garlic. Season with salt and pepper. Simmer gently for 30 minutes. Sift flour and salt into basin and add skim milk and remainder of oil. Stir with knife until it forms soft dough. Knead until dough is smooth and soft. Roll out and line a greased 9-inch pie pan. Fill with tomato mixture then top with anchovy fillets, sliced olives and cottage cheese. Bake in a moderate oven 40–45 minutes.

Per serving: 2 tablespoons oil   Serves 4

SAVORY PASTRY

2 cups flour	½ cup polyunsaturated oil
1 teaspoon salt	
½ cup ice water	

Sift flour and salt into bowl. Beat together oil and water until thickened. Pour all at once into flour and mix with fork until flour is entirely moistened. Form pastry into a ball. Cut in half and roll out one piece at a time between two sheets of waxed paper, rolling out lightly from center. Peel off top paper, lift paper and pastry by corners and place paper side up in an 8-inch pie pan. Remove remaining paper, ease pastry into pie pan. Fill with desired filling and repeat the above with second half of pastry. Seal the edges and flute; cut vents in top crust. Bake in hot oven for 15 minutes, reduce heat to moderate and continue baking 20 minutes longer (or according to time required for filling used). Enough pastry for two 8-inch tart shells or one double pie crust. Suggested fillings: Savory Mince; Salmon Wizz.

SPANISH TART

1½ cups flour
¼ teaspoon salt
½ cup polyunsaturated margarine
Cold water to mix
2 tablespoons polyunsaturated oil

¾ cup sliced onions
1 clove garlic, crushed
3 small zucchini, sliced
3 tomatoes, peeled and sliced
Salt and pepper
Chopped parsley

Sift flour and salt into bowl, rub margarine in lightly with fingertips. Sprinkle enough water over to mix to a firm dough. Knead lightly. Chill 30 minutes then roll out thinly on floured board to fit an 8-inch greased flan ring or pie pan. Bake in moderately hot oven for 12–15 minutes. Spanish Filling: Heat oil, add onions, garlic and zucchini. Fry lightly for 5 minutes (do not brown), add tomatoes and cook 3 minutes longer. Season to taste. Spoon hot filling into tart and serve sprinkled with parsley. Serve hot as a first course or for a light meal with a tossed salad.

Per serving: 2 teaspoons oil   Serves 4

One-Week Menu for Modified-Fat Diet

BREAKFAST	LUNCH	DINNER
SUNDAY		
Stewed peaches Oatmeal and filled milk (74) Baked beans in tomato sauce on toast	French onion soup (21) croutons (76) Roast seasoned leg lamb (33) Gravy. Scalloped potato (47) Roast pumpkin Broccoli Apple strudel (59) and ice cream (65)	Pizza pie (80) Tossed salad Fresh fruit
MONDAY		
Orange juice Oatmeal and filled milk (74) Broiled fish, lemon wedges	Cold seasoned lamb slices Italian salad (50) lettuce Fresh fruit or Packed lunch (see below)	Fish pie with herbs (24) Glazed potato balls (45) Minted peas Carrot straws Apricot crumble (63), custard (64)
TUESDAY		
Grapefruit Cereal and filled milk (74) Asparagus with parsley spread (70) on toast	Salmon wizz (26) Tomato slices Fresh fruit or Packed lunch of: Tomato, salmon and onion sandwiches Cottage cheese and cucumber sandwiches Fresh fruit	Corned beef, onion sauce (73) Boiled potatoes Cabbage Tomato scallop (48) Chocolate Sauce Pudding (62)

WEDNESDAY

Pineapple juice
Oatmeal and filled milk (74)
Spaghetti in tomato sauce on toast

Cold rump roast
Tomato, marinated cucumber (50)
Cottage cheese potato salad (50)
Fresh fruit or
Packed lunch (above or below)

Fried chicken pieces (78)
Mashed potato
Corn, beans
Creamed rice (64) & canned cherries

THURSDAY

Stewed prunes
Cereal and filled milk (74)
Broiled kippers and lemon juice, parsley spread (70)

Chilled tomato soup (19)
Peanut butter and celery sandwiches
Raisin and walnut (78) sandwiches
Fresh fruit or
Packed lunch (above or below)

Malaysian lamb curry (32)
Saffron rice (46)
Quick banana dessert (67)

FRIDAY

Fruit compote
Cereal and filled milk (74)
Sweet corn niblets on toast

Spanish tart (81)
Tossed salad & piquant sauce (71)
Fresh fruit or
Packed lunch of:
Tuna and gherkin sandwich (78)
Yogurt
Fresh fruit

Seasoned fillet of fish (27)
Baked jacket potatoes
Beans
Ice Cream (65) and fresh fruit salad

SATURDAY

Tomato juice
Cereal and filled milk (74)
Grilled tomato on toast

Spaghetti & meat sauce (35)
Cabbage salad (49)
Fresh fruit

Veal and potato casserole (38)
Corn, Brussels sprouts
Lemon meringue pie (66)

□4□

The Calorie-Restricted Diet

Losing weight is a slow process. You cannot hope to lose more than about 2 pounds per week, even though your initial weight loss may be more spectacular. A steady loss of 7 pounds per month is highly successful.

The essential feature of any diet is to eat less or exercise more or do both. Two diets are presented here. One is a simple scheme best suited to those who need to take off only a few pounds. The other is more rigid and detailed and is divided into two parts, depending on whether weight loss is to be combined with reduction of blood cholesterol.

Diets should be used only when there are no complicating factors. Diabetics, pregnant women, children, the severely overweight and those who have any sort of medical problem should consult their doctor before starting a diet. Also consult your doctor if you intend to reduce drastically or continue the diet for a long period of time.

A SIMPLE DIET

1. Eat less by consciously taking smaller helpings and cutting away any fat.

DESIRABLE WEIGHT ACCORDING TO HEIGHT AND SEX*

Men, 25 years and over

HEIGHT (with shoes on)		SMALL FRAME	MEDIUM FRAME	LARGE FRAME
Feet	Inches			
5	2	112–120	118–129	126–141
5	3	115–123	121–133	129–144
5	4	118–126	126–136	132–148
5	5	121–129	127–139	135–152
5	6	124–133	130–143	138–156
5	7	128–137	134–147	142–161
5	8	132–141	138–152	147–166
5	9	136–145	142–156	151–170
5	10	140–150	146–160	155–174
5	11	144–154	150–165	159–179
6	0	148–158	154–170	164–184
6	1	152–162	158–175	168–189
6	2	156–167	162–180	173–194
6	3	160–171	167–185	178–199
6	4	164–175	172–190	182–204

Women, 25 years and over

HEIGHT (with shoes on)		SMALL FRAME	MEDIUM FRAME	LARGE FRAME
Feet	Inches			
4	10	92–98	96–107	104–119
4	11	94–101	98–110	106–122
5	0	96–104	101–113	109–125
5	1	99–107	104–116	112–128
5	2	102–110	107–119	115–131
5	3	105–113	110–122	118–134
5	4	108–116	113–126	121–138
5	5	111–119	116–130	125–142
5	6	114–123	120–135	129–146
5	7	118–127	124–139	133–150
5	8	122–131	128–143	137–154
5	9	126–135	132–147	141–158
5	10	130–140	136–151	145–163
5	11	134–144	140–155	149–168
6	0	138–148	144–159	153–173

Figures provided by Metropolitan Life Insurance Company

2. Choose foods which supply fewer calories per serving.

3. Increase physical activity — walk to the next bus stop, walk upstairs, stand rather than sit, do exercises, take up sports. Patients with medical complications should check with their doctor.

4. Check progress by weighing weekly.

Protein, fat, carbohydrates and alcohol all supply calories or fuel for energy expenditure but fats are the richest source of calories. Fats include butter, cream, margarines, oils, lard, drippings and similar frying mediums. Food items which use both fat and carbohydrates in their preparation are rich in calories, e.g., fried foods, cakes, pastries, cookies. Beer, wines, sugar, sweetened cordials and soft drinks are not essential foods and they are often to blame for excess calories.

No foods are forbidden to you in this diet, but there should be a reduction in the number of times calorie-rich foods are eaten each week. If you elect to follow this type of diet then on most occasions you should substitute a lower-calorie food item for the higher-calorie food, i.e., broiled for fried meats; fruit for cookies, cakes and puddings; and spirits plus water or soda for beer.

1200-CALORIE-RESTRICTED DIETS

This diet is designed to provide fewer calories than are used in normal daily activities; strict adherence to it will certainly result in weight reduction. Some foods are prohibited (calorie-rich foods), some are limited (foods required to ensure an adequate intake of essential nutrients, i.e., protein, vitamins and minerals) and others are unrestricted (low-calorie foods).

Details of two diets, each of which provide 1200 calories per day, are given below. If you are concerned only with reducing weight then follow the dietary program outlined in Diet No. 1. (See also menu on page 119)

Diet No. 2 is to be followed if blood cholesterol is to be reduced at the same time. (See also menu on page 121.) The principles to be followed in this latter diet are the same as those outlined in the Modified-Fat Diet with the additional requirement of restricting your caloric intake. For further details of these principles read the section on the Modified-Fat Diet.

	DIET NO. 1	DIET NO. 2
MILK	½ pint whole milk	½ pint skim milk
EGG	One	None
BEEF, LAMB, PORK	2 portions	2 ounces
POULTRY, RABBIT, VEAL	5 ounces cooked weight	4 ounces
FISH	As a meat substitute	Same
CHEESE	As a meat or milk substitute	Only cottage cheese allowed as a meat or milk substitute
FRUIT	2 portions	Same
STARCHY VEGETABLES	3 portions	Same
NON-STARCHY VEGETABLES	As desired	Same
BREAD	3 ounces	Same
BUTTER	½ ounce	None
POLYUN-SATURATED MARGARINE		½ ounce
POLYUN-SATURATED OIL		½ ounce

FRUIT

Fruit and fruit juices contain carbohydrates in the form of sugars and if eaten in excess will supply extra calories. Use either fresh, stewed or canned fruit *without* sugar.

1 portion = 1 medium-sized apple, pear, orange, peach
2 medium-sized apricots, plums, nectarines
1 small banana or mango
12–14 cherries or grapes
3 ounces fruit juice
½ cup blackberries, fresh fruit salad, papaya or pineapple
(1 cup = 8 ounces standard measure cup)

The amount of sugar per portion in the following fruits is very low and so you may have one of them as an extra each day.

1 portion = ½ small grapefruit — no added sugar
1 average slice honeydew
1 large slice watermelon
1 glass tomato juice (6 ounces)
1 passion fruit

STARCHY VEGETABLES

Vegetables which contain a larger proportion of carbohydrates, in the form of starch or sugar, and consequently supply more calories are referred to as the starchy vegetables.

1 portion = ½ cup (3 ounces by weight) beets, Brussels sprouts, carrots, pumpkin
= ⅓ cup (2 ounces by weight) lentil beans, corn, parsnips, peas, potatoes

1 portion of fruit may be substituted for 1 portion of starchy vegetables.

NON-STARCHY VEGETABLES

These vegetables contain a low proportion of carbohydrates and therefore supply few calories per serving. They may be used several times each day to add variety and to satisfy hunger. They may also be used for between-meal snacks:

Asparagus, french beans, broccoli, cabbage, cauliflower, celery, Chinese cabbage, cucumber, eggplant, kale, kohlrabi, lettuce, marrow, mushrooms, onions, peppers (red or green), radishes, spinach, squash, tomato, turnips, watercress, zucchini.

SUBSTITUTIONS

Weight reduction takes time and a monotonous diet is both uninteresting and difficult to follow. There is no reason why you should not have a varied menu and at the time lose weight. Study the *substitutions* below and on most occasions a few adjustments should enable you to have the same food as the rest of your family.

Foods within the following groups may be substituted or exchanged for one another. Foods from *different* groups cannot be substituted because they differ in their content of protein, fat, carbohydrate and calories.

Milk substitutions:
¼ pint (5 ounces) whole milk = ½ pint skim milk
½ pint buttermilk
¼ pint unflavored yogurt
8 ounces unflavored non-fat yogurt
1 ounce cheese
3 ounces cottage cheese
2 ounces vanilla ice cream

¼ pint (5 ounces) skim milk = ¼ pint buttermilk
3½ ounces unflavored nonfat yogurt
2 ounces cottage cheese

Meat substitutes: All visible fat is to be removed *before cooking.* Prepare meats without *flour.* Use butter, polyunsaturated margarine or oil from *daily allowance* for cooking. No *extra* fats to be used.

1 ounce cooked meat = 3 ounces steamed fish, waterpack tuna or salmon
2 ounces ·fish + 1 teaspoon butter, polyunsaturated margarine or polyunsaturated oil
1 ounce oil-pack fish, such as sardine or tuna
1 ounce cheese (for use in Diet No. 1 only)
3 ounces cottage cheese
1 egg (for use in Diet No. 1 only)

FOODS NOT ALLOWED

Sugar, honey, jam, marmalade; dried fruits; hard candies, chocolates, cordials, syrups; nuts; cakes, pastries, biscuits, puddings, ice cream; flours, cornstarch, arrowroot, thickened soups, gravies and stews; salad dressings, mayonnaise, oil, cream; fried foods; peanut butter; spaghetti, macaroni, rice; alcoholic drinks.

FOODS ALLOWED IN UNLIMITED AMOUNTS

Bovril, clear broth (all fat removed), black tea or coffee, condiments, curry powder, essences, fish paste, herbs, junket tablets, lemon juice, low-calorie soft drinks, mustard powder, spices, saccharine, sugarless cordials, sugarless (diabetic) jelly, soda water, vinegar, Worcestershire sauce, non-starchy vegetables.

WHEN DINING OUT

Select menu from fruit juice or fruit cocktails, clear soup, broiled foods, salads (no dressing); fruit or cheese as dessert.

OTHER WEIGHT REDUCING PROGRAMS

Other programs which have been suggested at various times include fad diets, liquid diets, and even complete starvation in which only vitamins and calorie-free fluids are taken.

When and if complete starvation is undertaken it should only be under strict medical supervision. Complete starvation may cause a large loss of muscle and other protein-containing tissues and may also precipitate gout, peptic ulceration and other complications.

Fad diets include those diets based on a particular food such as eggs, bananas, etc. Fluid diets, whether based on fruit juices or commercially prepared mixtures, are similar to the fad diets in that they appeal to those people who like to try something different. These types of diets are not recommended because usually they do not supply adequate amounts of the essential nutrients which are required each day, they can only be tolerated for short periods and they do not train you in new food habits which you can continue after you attain your ideal body weight.

PROGRESS DURING WEIGHT REDUCTION

It is advisable not to weigh yourself more than once each week. Remember, as discussed earlier, that body weight can vary by as much as several pounds from one day to the next or even within the one day due to changes in the amount of water in the body. Therefore do not become depressed if your weight remains stationary or increases over short periods even though you have adhered strictly to your diet. The amount of fat in the body will have decreased — and this is the main objective of the program — and the general trend in body weight will be a reduction over the weeks and months. An average weekly loss of one to two pounds is as good as can be expected. There is no advantage in restricting salt or water (or non-calorie drinks) unless the doctor has ordered this for other reasons.

WHEN WEIGHT REDUCTION IS STOPPED

Once you reach your goal you can relax your diet but it is still advisable to keep weekly checks on your weight. Your aim now is to maintain this new weight. This means that you will be able to relax your diet and eat more. Introduce extra foods gradually, watching your weight, but preserve the general features of the new food habits which you have acquired. Cautiously add small amounts of items which you have particularly missed, e.g., a little more lean meat, maybe thickened gravy, extra fruit or vegetable, or a dessert or piece of cake. Sugar is not recommended for re-introduction because it supplies only calories. During the first six months or so in particular, you must be very careful that you do not revert to your former eating habits because if you do you will start regaining all the weight you have lost.

□5□
Recipes For Calorie-Restricted Diets

These recipes are included to show that meals on a Calorie-Restricted Diet need not be unappetizing. By a few adaptions such as omitting fats and thickening agents and reducing the amount of stock normally used, most of your favorite meat recipes become suitable for use while on this diet. No recipes have been included for cakes, cookies or fancy desserts because these are calorie-rich foods.

Information at the end of each recipe indicates if a substitution of one portion of fruit, starchy vegetable or meat, etc. is required per serving. For example *"Substitution:* 1 portion meat" means that each serving of that particular dish is equivalent to one of the two portions of meat allowed per day in the Calorie-Restricted Diet. *"Substitution:* Free" means there is no restriction on the number of servings eaten each day.

SOUPS

ASPARAGUS SOUP

One 8½-ounce can
asparagus cuts
¼ cup diced cooked
chicken
2 cups water

½ cup asparagus liquid
3 chicken bouillon
cubes
1 teaspoon brandy or
sherry (optional)

Salt and pepper

Combine all ingredients, bring to boil.

Substitution: Free   Serves 4

CELERY SOUP

2 cups finely chopped
celery
2 teaspoons vegetable
concentrate, if avail-
able

Salt and pepper
4 cups beef stock

Add chopped celery, vegetable concentrate, salt and
pepper to stock and heat gently for 10 minutes.

Substitution: Free   Serves 4

CHILLED BUTTERMILK SOUP

2 cups tomato juice
2 cups chilled butter-
milk

Chopped chives or
shallots

Salt and pepper

Blend juice and buttermilk, add chives or shallots.
Season to taste. Chill.

Substitution: ½ cup skim milk   Serves 4

94

CHINESE CHICKEN SOUP

¼ cup strips of raw
   chicken
2 teaspoons salt
4-6 dried mushrooms

4 cups chicken stock
2 teaspoons soy sauce
1 tablespoon lemon
   juice

Chopped chives

Sprinkle chicken strips with salt and set aside. Add dried mushrooms to 1 cup hot chicken stock and set aside. Add remainder of stock to saucepan with soy sauce and bring to boil. Remove mushrooms from stock and cut into thin strips. Add mushrooms, chicken strips and stock to remainder of stock and simmer for 5–10 minutes. Add lemon juice and chives and simmer 5 minutes longer.

Substitution: Free   Serves 4

JULIENNE SOUP

½ cup sliced onions
¼ cup sliced carrots
¼ cup diced turnips
4 cups beef stock

½ cup green beans
   (cooked or canned)
Salt and pepper to
   taste

Simmer onions, carrots and turnips in the stock until tender. Add beans and salt and pepper to taste.

Substitution: Free   Serves 4

TOMATO CONSOMME

2 cups tomato juice
1 beef bouillon cube

1 cup water
Dash lemon juice

Salt and pepper to taste

Combine all ingredients, heat until bouillon cube is dissolved, serve piping hot.

Substitution: Free   Serves 4

FISH

BAKED FISH

1½ pounds fish fillets
1 tablespoon lemon
  juice
1½ cups sliced tomatoes

¾ cup onion rings
Salt and pepper
Pinch mixed herbs
(optional)

Place fish on large piece of foil and sprinkle with lemon juice. Top with tomato slices, onion rings, salt, pepper and herbs. Fold edges of foil tightly, place on oiled baking sheet in moderate oven for 15–20 minutes or until fish flakes easily.

Substitution: 1 portion meat   Serves 4

MARINATED BAKED FISH

1½ pounds fish fillets
2 small cloves garlic,
  thinly sliced
¼ teaspoon pepper

1 teaspoon salt
2 tablespoons chopped
  parsley
½ cup white vinegar

Arrange fillets in baking dish. Combine garlic with pepper, salt and parsley, mix gradually with vinegar and pour over fish. Let stand 1 hour. Bake in moderate oven 15–20 minutes.

Substitution: 1 portion meat   Serves 4

QUICK SALMON SNACK

2 tablespoons Worcestershire sauce
4 tablespoons Tomato
  Sauce (p. 115) or
  tomato puree
2 teaspoons chili sauce

1 teaspoon cayenne
  pepper
Salt
1-pound can or 2
  cups salmon

Combine all sauce ingredients, stir well. Drain and flake salmon and fold through sauce. Place in fancy mold or bowl and chill. May also be served hot.

Substitution: 1 portion meat   Serves 4

SALMON AND TOMATO SAVORY

2 cups chopped tomato
½ cup onion rings
1 tablespoon lemon
   juice
½ cup pepper rings
½ teaspoon mustard

¼ teaspoon pepper
½ teaspoon salt
1½ teaspoons chopped
   parsley
1-pound can salmon or
   tuna

Mix tomatoes, onions, lemon juice, pepper rings, mustard, pepper, salt and parsley. Cook until tender. Add flaked salmon. Simmer until salmon is heated, about 5–10 minutes.

Substitution: 1 portion meat   Serves 4

SOUSED FISH

1½ pounds fish fillets
1 cup sliced onion
6 peppercorns
6 cloves

2 bay leaves
1 teaspoon salt
¾ cup vinegar
¾ cup water

1 head lettuce

Place fish in a baking dish and cover with sliced onion. Add dry ingredients, then the vinegar and water and cover with greased paper. Bake in a moderately hot oven 30 minutes. Let fish stand in liquid until set then lift out fish carefully and place in center of serving dish. Strain liquid over fish and garnish with lettuce leaves.

Substitution: 1 portion meat   Serves 4

MEATS

BRAISED CHOPS

1 pound lean loin lamb
  chops
½ cup chopped celery
1 cup chopped onion
½ cup chopped green
  pepper
1 bay leaf

2 teaspoons vinegar
2 teaspoons soy sauce
½ cup beef stock
Salt and pepper to
  taste
1 tablespoon chopped
  parsley

Trim fat from chops. Arrange in baking dish. Add celery, onion, peppers, bay leaf, vinegar, soy sauce, stock, salt and pepper. Bake in moderate oven for approximately 2 hours or until the chops are tender. Serve sprinkled with parsley.

Substitution: 1 portion meat   Serves 4

BRAISED STEAK

1 pound round steak
1 cup chopped onions
1 cup chopped celery
½ cup chopped green
  pepper

1 cup chopped
  tomatoes
½ cup stock
½ teaspoon salt

Trim fat from meat, cut into serving pieces and place in casserole. Add vegetables and stock. Season. Cook in a moderate oven until meat is tender; add more stock if required.

Substitution: 1 portion meat   Serves 4

INDIAN BEEF MARINADE

2 teaspoons powdered
   coriander
1 teaspoon cumin
2 teaspoons turmeric
1½ tablespoons green
   ginger cut as match
   sticks or ¼ teaspoon
   ground ginger

2 cloves garlic, crushed
2 cups chopped onions
¾ cup vinegar
1 pound lean top
   round steak cut into
   thin strips
1 bay leaf
Salt

Mix together spices, crushed garlic and onions and blend into vinegar. Pour over beef slices and allow to marinate for 24 hours, turning often. Simmer meat in marinade until tender.

Substitution: 1 portion meat

Serves 4

MEAT SAUCE

1 pound ground meat
½ cup chopped onion
1 clove garlic
½ cup chopped green
   pepper

1 bay leaf
1 cup tomato juice or 1
   cup chopped tomatoes
¼ teaspoon pepper
½ teaspoon salt

Heat pan. Add meat, stirring constantly until it changes color. Add onion, garlic and peppers and cook 5 minutes longer. Add bay leaf, tomato juice (or tomatoes), pepper and salt and cook gently for 20–30 minutes. Set aside to cool. Skim fat off. Reheat to serve.

Substitution: 1 portion meat

Serves 4

MEXICAN RICE*

1 pound lean chuck
steak, ground
½ cup uncooked rice
¾ cup thinly sliced
onion
1 small clove garlic,
crushed
2 teaspoons salt

1 tablespoon chili
powder or Tomato
Chutney (p. 116)
⅓ cup Tomato Sauce
(p. 115)
½ pound skinned,
roughly chopped
tomatoes

1 cup water or stock

Place meat, rice, onion and garlic in saucepan and stir
continuously until meat is brown. Add salt, chili powder,
tomato sauce, tomatoes and water; stir well. Cover,
simmer 25 minutes, stirring occasionally or until rice is
tender.

Substitution: 1 portion meat + 1 slice bread   Serves 4

STEAK DIANE

1 pound rump steak,
thinly sliced
3 tablespoons Worces-
tershire sauce

6 tablespoons tomato
juice
1½ tablespoons vinegar
1 tablespoon chopped
parsley

Sear steak quickly on both sides in large frying pan. Mix
Worcestershire sauce, tomato juice and vinegar. Add to
pan and bring to boil. Simmer uncovered until meat is
tender and liquid has reduced. Sprinkle with chopped
parsley before serving.

Substitution: 1 portion meat   Serves 4

*When using recipe for Restricted-Calorie Diet No. 2, fry rice in
¼ cup polyunsaturated oil then continue as above.
Substitution: 1 portion of meat + 1 slice of bread + 1 tablespoon
oil

VEAL MARENGO

1½ pounds veal
1 clove garlic, crushed
1 cup small tomato wedges
1 cup fine onion wedges
1 small can button mushrooms

2 teaspoons tomato paste
½ cup white wine and ½ cup chicken stock, or 1 cup chicken stock
1 tablespoon chopped parsley

Cut veal into serving pieces. Place in casserole. Add garlic, tomato, onion, mushrooms, tomato paste, wine and chicken stock. Cover and cook in moderate oven until tender — approximately 1½ hours; garnish with parsley.

Substitution: 1 portion meat   Serves 4

POULTRY AND GAME

CHICKEN IN WINE

One 2½-pound chicken, cut up
1 tablespoon lemon juice
1 teaspoon salt
¼ teaspoon freshly ground black pepper

1 cup dry white wine
1 tablespoon chopped chives or onions
1 tablespoon parsley
Pinch dried thyme
Pinch dried tarragon

Wash and dry the chicken and rub with lemon juice. Season with salt and pepper. Place chicken pieces, wine, chopped chives, parsley, thyme and tarragon in casserole dish. Cover and cook in moderate oven until chicken is tender.

Substitution: 1 portion meat   Serves 4

DEVILLED CHICKEN

2½ pounds chicken
½ cup chopped onion
½ cup chopped carrot
½ cup chopped turnip

Bouquet garni
(parsley, thyme,
marjoram and bay
leaf tied together
with string)

Simmer chicken with vegetables and bouquet garni until tender. Leave in the cooking liquid until cold, then skin, joint and remove leg bones, slice into convenient pieces. Lay pieces in a casserole, pour Devil Sauce over (below) to moisten and place in a moderate oven. Heat for 15 minutes.

DEVIL SAUCE

3 tablespoons Worcestershire sauce
2 tablespoons button mushrooms
1 tablespoon tarragon vinegar
1 tablespoon finely chopped onions
2 or 3 slices lemon cut in half

1 clove garlic, crushed
1 teaspoon salt
1 cup strong chicken stock
1 cup canned or fresh peeled and chopped tomatoes
Freshly ground black pepper
1 bay leaf

Simmer these ingredients 10 minutes, pour over chicken while hot.

Substitution: 1 portion meat

Serves 4

HAWAIIAN CHICKEN

¼ teaspoon salt
¼ teaspoon pepper
2 teaspoons dry
mustard
¼ teaspoon nutmeg
One 2- to 2½-pound
chicken, cut up
1 cup chopped onions

2 tablespoons vinegar
1-pound can
unsweetened pine-
apple chunks or 2
cups fresh pineapple
chunks
1 cup chicken stock
1 tablespoon parsley

Mix salt, pepper, mustard, nutmeg and rub over chicken pieces. Place in casserole, add onion, vinegar, pineapple and stock. Cook in moderate oven until meat is tender, about 1½—2 hours. Garnish with parsley.
Substitution: 1 portion meat + 1 portion fruit   Serves 4

VEGETABLES

BAKED ONIONS

4 medium onions,
peeled

½ cup chicken stock
Salt and pepper

Arrange prepared onions in baking dish and pour chicken stock over. Sprinkle with salt and pepper. Bake in moderate oven until tender.
Substitution: Free   Serves 4

VARIATION
Potato or pumpkin may be cooked by this method.
Substitution: 1 portion vegetable

SAVORY MACARONI

⅔ cup macaroni
2 cups chopped tomatoes
¼ cup chopped green pepper

¼ cup chopped onion
1 clove garlic, crushed
Salt and pepper
1 tablespoon chopped parsley

Cook macaroni in salted water. Drain. Cook tomatoes, pepper, onions and garlic together until soft. Season with salt and pepper. Mix sauce through macaroni and garnish with parsley.

Substitution: 1 slice bread   Serves 4

VARIATION
Rice or spaghetti may be substituted for macaroni.

STUFFED TOMATOES

4 large tomatoes
½ cup cooked fish, salmon or tuna

½ cup chopped onion
¼ cup chopped celery
Pinch tarragon

Salt and pepper

Cut top off tomatoes and scoop out centers. Add cooked fish, onion, celery, tarragon, salt and pepper to tomato pulp. Fill tomatoes with required amount of mixture and bake in moderate oven for 10–15 minutes.

Substitution: Free

VARIATION
The flaked fish may be replaced by:

Minced-stuffed tomato: ½ cup chopped cold meat or ½ cup lean ground beef.

Substitution: 2 tablespoons meat

Anchovy-stuffed tomato: 4 anchovy fillets chopped + 1 tablespoon parsley.
Substitution: Free

Mushroom-stuffed tomato: 1 cup chopped mushrooms.
Substitution: Free

TOMATO AND ONION CASSEROLE

**3 large or 6 small   1 cup thin onion rings
  tomatoes   1 teaspoon dried herbs
          Salt and pepper**

Wash and slice tomatoes. Place layer of tomatoes in ovenproof dish, cover with onions, sprinkle with herbs, salt and pepper and repeat layers until dish is filled. Bake in moderate oven until vegetables are soft.
Substitution: Free   Serves 4

SALADS

BEAN SALAD

**2 cups sliced french   3 tablespoons malt
  beans   vinegar
1 teaspoon mustard
  seeds
          3 tablespoons water**

Cook beans and mustard seeds in boiling salted water. Drain. Combine vinegar and water, pour over beans, chill.
Substitution: Free   Serves 4

COLESLAW

3 cups finely shredded
cabbage
¼ cup finely shredded
green pepper
¼ cup grated onion

¼ cup grated radish
1 teaspoon salt
¼ teaspoon pepper
Spiced Dressing
(p. 114)

Toss cabbage lightly with green pepper, onion, radish, salt, pepper and dressing.

Substitution: Free   Serves 4

GREEN BEAN RING

1 envelope gelatin
¼ cup cold water
1½ cups stock or water
2 teaspoons white
vinegar
2 teaspoons lemon juice

½ teaspoon garlic salt
¼ teaspoon pepper
½ teaspoon salt
¼ cup chopped celery
1¾ cups cooked cut
green beans

Soften gelatin in water. Place stock in saucepan with vinegar, lemon juice, garlic salt, pepper, salt and celery. Heat gently until boiling then remove from heat and add softened gelatin, stir until dissolved. Add cooked beans, pour into 7-inch ring mold or 4 small ring molds. Chill 1 hour or until set. Run knife around edges to loosen.

Substitution: Free   Serves 4

GREEN CABBAGE RELISH

½ large green cabbage
2 large onions
Salt
2 cups vinegar

Liquid sweetener to
taste
1 teaspoon mustard
2 teaspoons curry
powder

Clean cabbage and shred. Peel and slice onions thinly. Fold through cabbage and sprinkle with enough salt to coat well and leave for 24 hours. Drain and rinse thoroughly and then put in vinegar to which sweetener, mustard and curry powder have been added. Bring to boil and allow to simmer for 20 minutes. Bottle and seal. Serve with broiled meat and salads.

Substitution: Free   Makes 1–1½ pints

PICKLED CUCUMBERS

4 large cucumbers   **Spiced Vinegar**
  Brine (1½ pounds salt   **(p. 114)**
  to 4 cups water)

Slice cucumber, with skin on, very thinly. Quarter each slice or if cucumber is small, leave in rings. Soak cucumber in the brine for 24 hours. Drain thoroughly then pack tightly into jars. Pour hot Spiced Vinegar to cover and seal in screwtop jars.

Substitution: Free

PICKLED ONIONS

4 pounds small white   **2 tablespoons mixed**
  onions   **spices**
½ cup salt   **2 pints white vinegar**
  Liquid sweetener to
  taste

Peel onions and put into a basin. Sprinkle with salt and leave to stand overnight. Rinse them thoroughly and dry as well as possible. Put sweetener, salt, spices and vinegar into saucepan and bring to boil. Add onions, cover and boil briskly for 4–5 minutes, or until soft. Pour into bottles and cover with airtight lids.

Substitution: Free

PICKLED RED CABBAGE

½ large red cabbage   Salt
Spiced Vinegar (p. 114)

Shred cabbage finely. Wash thoroughly and place shreds into a deep bowl and sprinkle with layers of salt. Leave for 24 hours. Wash and drain thoroughly. Pour hot Spiced Vinegar over cabbage and leave for a further 24 hours, stirring at intervals. Pack into jars and cover with airtight lid.

Substitution: Free

PINEAPPLE AND GRAPEFRUIT SALAD

2 cups crushed pine-apple
½ cup grapefruit sections

2 or 3 sprigs mint, chopped
2 tablespoons chopped green pepper (optional)

Mix pineapple, grapefruit, mint and green pepper. Chill mixture for at least 1 hour before serving.

Substitution: 1 portion fruit   Serves 4

RICE SALAD

2 cups cooked rice
½ cup finely sliced celery
¼ cup grated onion

¼ cup chopped radish
2 tablespoons chopped mint
2 teaspoons salt

¼ teaspoon pepper

Combine all ingredients. Chill.

Substitution: 1 slice bread   Serves 4

TOMATO SALAD

¼ cup vinegar
¼ cup water
1 teaspoon caraway
seeds

Salt and pepper
4 tomatoes, sliced
½ cup sliced onion

Combine vinegar, water, caraway seeds, salt and pepper and pour over tomato and onion. Chill.

Substitution: Free

DESSERTS

APPLE MILK JELLY

2 teaspoons gelatin
2 tablespoons hot water
Liquid sweetener to
taste

1 cup unsweetened
apple sauce
2 cups skim milk

Dissolve gelatin in hot water. Add artifical sweetener to apple sauce. Mix skim milk with apple and gelatin. Refrigerate to set.

Substitution: 1 portion fruit; 5 ounces skim milk

Serves 4

BAKED APPLE

4 medium cooking apples
Cloves
Spices, (Cinnamon,
Nutmeg, etc.)

Liquid sweetener to
taste
Lemon juice

Core apples. Place a couple of cloves in each apple and spices in centers. Place apples in baking dish with water, sweetener, lemon juice and bake slowly until tender, basting occasionally.

Substitution: 1 portion fruit

Serves 4

VARIATION

Pears or peaches may be substituted for apples

FRUIT SALAD

1 medium orange, sectioned	1 small banana, sliced
1 medium apple, sliced	½ cup crushed pineapple

Mix all fruit. Chill.

Substitution: 1 portion fruit   Serves 4

JELLIED APPLE SNOW

1 tablespoon gelatin	2 egg whites
4 tablespoons hot water	Liquid sweetener to taste
1 cup unsweetened apple sauce	Dash lemon juice

Soften gelatin in a little hot water and add to apple sauce. Cool. Fold in stiffly beaten egg whites. Add sweetener and lemon juices. Turn into serving dish and allow to set.

Substitution: 1 portion fruit   Serves 4

JELLIED PEACHES

5 medium peaches or 1-pound can unsweetened peaches, drained	1 cup diabetic jelly

Distribute fruit evenly in dish. Pour in jelly and set.

Substitution: 1 portion fruit   Serves 4

VARIATIONS

Any variety of unsweetened canned fruit or fresh fruit may be substituted for peaches. Use quantity equivalent to 4 servings.

JUNKET

⅓ cup dried skim milk   1½ cups water
  powder   Liquid sweetener to
2 junket tablets   taste
           2 teaspoons vanilla

Warm milk to lukewarm. Crush junket tablets and dissolve in a little water. Add crushed junket tablets, sweetener, vanilla to skim milk and pour into dish, sprinkle with nutmeg. Place aside to set.

Substitution: 5 ounces skim milk   Serves 4

VARIATION
Coffee: Add 1 tablespoon powdered instant coffee to skim milk.

MOCHA SPONGE

2 teaspoons gelatin   Liquid sweetener to
¼ cup water   taste
¾ cup boiling coffee   2 egg whites

Soften gelatin in water. Add coffee and sweetener and stir until dissolved. Leave until slightly thickened and then add stiffly beaten egg whites. Whisk until foamy. Chill.

Substitution: Free   Serves 4

VARIATIONS
Flummery: Substitute 8 ounces diluted calorie-free cordial for water and coffee.

ORANGE AND PINEAPPLE DELIGHT

1 cup unsweetened
pineapple pieces
plus liquid
1 tablespoon gelatin
6 tablespoons orange
juice
6 tablespoons cold water

2 tablespoons lemon
juice
Liquid sweetener to
taste
1 orange peeled and
cut into segments

Drain pineapple juice and soak gelatin in it. Bring orange juice and water to boil, add to gelatin, stir until dissolved. Add lemon juice and sweetener. Chill until setting then add pineapple and orange segments. Chill until set.

Substitution: 1 portion fruit   Serves 4

ORANGE CREAM

1 envelope gelatin
1⅓ cups orange juice
Liquid sweetener to
taste

⅓ cup nonfat milk
powder
¼ cup iced water

Dissolve gelatin in hot juice. Add sweetener, stir well and set aside to chill until the mixture begins to set. Sprinkle milk powder on iced water and beat until stiff. Fold into gelatin mixture and chill until set.

Substitution: 1 portion fruit; 5 ounces skim milk

Serves 4

PINEAPPLE DESSERT

1½ cups unsweetened
crushed pineapple
2 teaspoons gelatin
Liquid sweetener to
taste

¼ teaspoon grated
lemon rind
1 teaspoon vanilla
2 teaspoons lemon juice
Salt

1 cup skim milk

Drain pineapple. Reserve pineapple juice and water to make ½ cup. Sprinkle gelatin over pineapple juice. Allow to stand 5 minutes then dissolve over low heat. Remove and stir in sweetener, lemon rind, vanilla, lemon juice, salt, skim milk and drained pineapple. Chill.

Substitution: 1 portion fruit   Serves 4

PINEAPPLE MINT SHERBET

1 envelope gelatin
½ cup water
1 cup unsweetened
   pineapple juice
½ cup unsweetened
   crushed pineapple

1 tablespoon chopped
   fresh mint
2 teaspoons lemon juice
2 egg whites
Liquid sweetener to
   taste

Soften gelatin in water then add pineapple juice and pineapple, heat until gelatin has dissolved. Allow to cool, add chopped mint and lemon juice. Chill 1 hour. Beat egg whites until stiff and fold carefully through pineapple mixture. Sweeten if desired. Pour into rinsed mold and allow to chill until firm.

Substitution: 1 portion fruit   Serves 4

SAUCES AND DRESSINGS

MINT SAUCE

3 tablespoons hot water
2 tablespoons finely
   chopped mint

1 teaspoon liquid
   sweetener
3 tablespoons vinegar

Pour hot water over mint, add sweetener and vinegar. Stir and set aside until cold.

Substitution: Free   Makes ½ cup

CURRIED SAUCE

2 teaspoons curry
  powder
1 cup sliced onion
½ cup sliced green
  peppers
1 clove garlic

1 tablespoon chopped
  green ginger or 1
  teaspoon ground
  ginger
Juice of 1 lemon
1½ cups tomato juice

Heat pan to medium; add curry and onion and stir for
few minutes until golden. Add peppers, garlic, ginger,
lemon juice and tomato juice and simmer gently until
vegetables are soft. (For curried meat: pour over prepared meat, bake in moderate oven until meat is tender.)
Substitution: Free

SPICED DRESSING

2 tablespoons water
¼ cup tarragon vinegar
1 tablespoon minced
  chives
1 tablespoon chopped
  parsley

½ teaspoon salt
¼ teaspoon pepper
½ teaspoon paprika
¼ teaspoon oregano
Dash lemon juice

Mix ingredients. Chill in refrigerator to blend flavors.
Stir before serving.
Substitution: Free   Makes ½ cup

SPICED VINEGAR FOR PICKLING

¼ ounce mace
2 tablespoons allspice
2 tablespoons cloves
¼ stick cinnamon

6 peppercorns
3½ cups vinegar
Liquid sweetener to
  taste

Tie all the spices in a muslin bag. Pour the vinegar into a saucepan. Add spices. Cover the pan and bring the vinegar slowly to a boil. Simmer for a few minutes, remove the pan from the stove, add sweetener and leave to stand 1 hour. Lift out the spice bag. The vinegar is ready for immediate use if required.

Substitution: Free   Makes 1¾ pints

TOMATO DRESSING

One 12-ounce can tomato juice, 1½ cups
Juice of 1 lemon
½ cup white vinegar
2 cloves garlic, crushed

1 tablespoon finely chopped chives
3-4 drops Tabasco sauce

Combine all ingredients, shake well and chill. Store in refrigerator.

Substitution: Free   Makes 2 cups

TOMATO SAUCE

6 pounds tomatoes
1 pound onions
6 garlic cloves

⅓ cup salt
½ ounce cloves
½ ounce ground ginger

1 cup vinegar

Chop tomatoes and onions roughly. Add minced garlic, salt, cloves and ground ginger tied in muslin. Boil gently about 2 hours. Strain into saucepan, add vinegar and simmer until thick. Bottle and seal.

Substitution: Free

TOMATO CHUTNEY

4 pounds ripe tomatoes
2 green peppers,
chopped
4 chopped chili
peppers
1½ cups chopped celery
1½ cups chopped onion
Liquid sweetener to
taste

2 teaspoons Tabasco
sauce
1 tablespoon salt
1½ cups cider vinegar
1 stick cinnamon
1 teaspoon whole
cloves
1½ teaspoons mustard
seed

1½ teaspoons celery seed

Pour boiling water over tomatoes, peel and chop. In large saucepan combine tomatoes, peppers, celery, onion, liquid sweetener, Tabasco, salt and vinegar. Tie spices in muslin bag and add to tomato mixture. Bring to a boil. Reduce heat and simmer, stirring occasionally until of desired consistency (approximately 2 hours). Pour into hot sterilized jars. Seal at once.

Substitution: Free   Makes 4 cups

YOGURT SALAD DRESSING

1 clove garlic, crushed
1 teaspoon mustard
1 teaspoon paprika

1 tablespoon vinegar
1 jar or container non-
fat yogurt

Mix garlic, mustard and paprika with vinegar. Mix thoroughly with yogurt. Let stand 2 hours before using.
Substitution: 1 tablespoon free   Makes 1 cup

ZERO SALAD DRESSING

1 cup tomato juice   2 tablespoons finely
¼ cup lemon juice   chopped onion
¼ teaspoon pepper

Mix all ingredients. Store in refrigerator. Shake before using.

Substitution: Free   Makes 1⅛ cups

BEVERAGES

LEMON TINGLE

Ice cubes   2 large bottles soda
Juice of 4 lemons   water (26 ounces)
1 teaspoon powdered   Liquid sweetener to
   ginger or sliced green   taste
   ginger

Place ice cubes in jug. Add lemon, powdered ginger, soda water and sweetener. Mix well and serve immediately.

Substitution: Free   Serves 4

SPARKLING MINT TEA

2 cups strong tea   ½ cup lemon juice
   Liquid sweetener to   1 cup or ½ pint chilled
   taste   soda water
Mint

Strain tea, add liquid sweetener. Let stand until cold. Stir in lemon juice, add soda water and serve in tall glasses with ice, mint and lemon slices.

Substitution: Free   Makes 3½ cups

SPICED TEA

⅛ teaspoon nutmeg	¼ cup orange juice
⅛ teaspoon allspice	¼ cup lemon juice
⅛ teaspoon cinnamon	2 cups cold water
2 cups hot water	Liquid sweetener to
1 tablespoon tea	taste

Tie spices securely in muslin bag, add hot water, boil 1 minute. Pour over tea leaves and steep 3 minutes. Strain, then add fruit juices and cold water. Chill. Add liquid sweetener according to taste and serve very cold.

Substitution: Free   Makes 4½ cups

TOMATO COOLER

1½ cups tomato juice	2 drops Tabasco sauce
¼ cup finely chopped	1 tablespoon lemon
celery	juice
2 teaspoons soy sauce	

Combine all ingredients, add salt to taste if desired. Chill until ready to serve.

Substitution: Free   Serves 4

One-Week Menus
Calorie-Restricted Diet

DIET NO. 1 (See also p. 87)

BREAKFAST	LUNCH	DINNER
SUNDAY		
Fruit juice (1PV)	Roast leg lamb,	Salmon and tomato
Cereal (1B) and	mint sauce (113)	savory (97)
milk	Roast potato (103)	Rice (1B)
Scrambled egg	(1PV)	Fresh fruit (1PF)
Toast (1B)	Roast pumpkin	
	(103) (1PV)	
	Broccoli	
	Pineapple dessert	
	(112) (1PF)	
MONDAY		
Cereal (1B) and	Cold lamb slices	Chicken in wine
milk	Coleslaw (106) zero	(101)
1 poached egg	dressing (117)	Boiled potato (2PV)
Toast (1B)	Asparagus	Brussels sprouts
	Bread (1B)	(1PV)
	Fresh fruit (1PF)	Savory stuffed
	or Packed lunch	tomato (104)
	(below)	Jellied apple snow
		(110) (1PF)
TUESDAY		
Tomato juice	1 cheese and lettuce	Broiled steak
Cod, lemon wedges	sandwich (2B)	Mashed potato
Toast (1B)	Celery curls	(1PV)
	Fresh fruit (2PF)	Carrot straws (1PV)
	or Packed lunch	Cauliflower and
	(below)	parsley
		Orange and pine-
		apple delight (112)
		(1PF-1PV)

WEDNESDAY

½ grapefruit
1 boiled egg
Toast (1B)

Soused fish (97)
Tossed salad
Wholewheat bread
(2B)
Fresh fruit (1PF)
or
Packed lunch of:
1 salmon and celery
sandwich (2B)
1 fresh fruit (1PF)

Hawaiian chicken
(103) (1PF-1PV)
Boiled rice
(1B-2PV)
Beans
Junket (111)
Unsweetened
canned apricots
(1PF)

THURSDAY

Pineapple juice
(1PV)
1 poached egg
Toast (1B)

Chinese chicken
soup (95)
Cottage cheese
Rice salad (108)
(1B) yogurt salad
dressing (116)
Tomato salad (109)
Lettuce
Wholewheat bread
(1B)
Fresh fruit (1PF)
or
Packed lunch
(above)

Steak Diane (100)
Baked jacket potato
(1PV)
Lima beans (1PV)
Cauliflower
Orange cream (112)
(1PF)

FRIDAY

Cereal (1B) +
milk
Grilled cheese toast
(1B)

1 stuffed curried egg
Sardines
Celery curls,
cucumber, tomato
Bread (1B)
Fresh fruit (1PF-
1PV)
or
Packed lunch
(above)

Corned beef
Mashed potato
(1PV)
Carrots (1PV)
Onions
Fresh fruit salad
(110) (2PF)

SATURDAY

Tomato omelette	Cold corned beef	Celery soup (94)
Toast (2B)	slices	Baked marinated
	Coleslaw (106)	fish (96) lemon
	spiced dressing (114)	wedges
	Cucumber and	Parsley steamed
	onion salad	potato (1PV)
	Wholewheat bread	Peas (2PV)
	(1B)	Flummery (111)
	Fresh fruit (1PF)	Unsweetened
		canned peaches
		(1PF)

1PV = equivalent to 1 portion of starchy vegetable
1PF = equivalent to 1 portion of fruit
1B = equivalent to 1 slice bread
Menu items marked with one of the above symbols show how the use of
substitutions *can add variety to your diet.*

DIET NO. 2 (See also p. 87)

BREAKFAST	**LUNCH**	**DINNER**

SUNDAY

Pineapple juice	Celery soup (94)	Meat sauce (99)
(1PF-1PV)	Roast chicken	and spaghetti (1B)
Cereal (1B) skim	Roast potato (103)	Tossed salad and
milk	(1PV)	tarragon dressing
Stewed tomato and	Roast pumpkin	(71) (0)
onion	(103) (1PV)	Fresh fruit (1PF)
Toast (1B)	Beans	
	Orange and pine-	
	apple delight (102)	
	(1PF)	

MONDAY

Cereal (1B) skim milk
Asparagus
Toast (1B)

Cold Chicken
Rice salad (108) (1B)
Yogurt salad dressing (116)
Tomato slices, lettuce
Fresh fruit (1PF)

Grilled fish (25)
(0) lemon wedges
Mashed potato (2PV)
Corn (1PV)
Broccoli
Mocha sponge (111)
Unsweetened canned pears (1PF)

TUESDAY

Tomato juice
Corn niblets (1PV)
Toast (1B)

Quick salmon snack (96)
Coleslaw (106)
Piquant sauce (71) (0)
Wholewheat bread (2B)
Fresh fruit (1PF)
or
Packed lunch of:
1 salmon and cucumber sandwich (2B)
Coleslaw (106)
Piquant sauce (71) (0)
Fresh fruit (1PF)

Corned leg of mutton
Potato (1PV)
Carrot (1PV)
Cabbage
Pineapple mint sherbet (113) (1PF)

WEDNESDAY

Grapefruit
Cereal (1B) and filled milk (74) (0)
Toast (1B)

Corned mutton slices
Green bean ring (106)
Radishes, lettuce
Bread (1B)
Fresh fruit (1PF)

Julienne soup (95)
Veal Marengo (101)
Poppy seed macaroni (2PV)
Peas (1PV)
Cauliflower
Flummery (111)
Unsweetened canned apricots (1PF)

THURSDAY

Orange juice (1PF)
Cereal (1B) and
filled milk (74) (0)
Toast (1B)

Salmon and tomato
savory (97)
Celery
Wholewheat bread
(1B)
Fresh fruit (1PF)
or
Packed lunch of:
Salmon
Celery, tomato,
asparagus
Wholewheat bread
(1B)
Fresh fruit (1PF)

Braised chops (98)
Baked jacket potato
(1PV)
Pumpkin (1PV)
Spinach
Jellied fruit (110)
(1PF-1PV)

FRIDAY

Grapefruit
Cod and lemon
wedges
Toast (1B)

Cottage cheese and
walnut (0)
Radish, tomato,
lettuce
Fresh fruit (1PF)
Bread (2B)

Baked fish (96)
Mashed potato
(2PV)
Carrot straws (1PV)
Beans
Baked apple (109)
(1PF)

SATURDAY

Cereal (1B) skim
milk
Corn niblets with
tomato (1PV)
Toast (1B)

Asparagus soup
(94)
Mexican rice (100)
(1B) (0)
Salad and spiced
dressing (114)
Fresh fruit (1PF)

Curried chicken
(114)
Tomato chutney
(116)
Mashed potato
(1PV)
Peas (1PV)
Jellied apple snow
(110) (1PF)

1PV = equivalent to 1 portion of starchy vegetable
0   = equivalent to ½ ounce polyunsaturated oil
1PF = equivalent to 1 portion of fruit
1B = equivalent to 1 slice bread
Menu items marked with one of the above symbols show how the use of
substitutions *can add variety to your diet.*

INDEX

A

Apple cake, 53
Apple milk jelly, 109
Apple strudel, 59
Asparagus soup, 94

B

Baked apple, 109
Baked apple roll, 61
Baked fish, 22, 96
Baked fish, marinated, 96
Baked onions, 103
Banana dessert, quick, 67
Banana flambé, 61
Barbecue fish, 23
Barbecue sauce, 69
Basic cream soup, 19
Bean salad, 105
Beef in Burgundy, 30
Beverages:
    Buttermilk punch, 74
    Coffee, iced, 75
    Introduction to, 73
    Lemon tingle, 117
    Milk, filled, 74
    Milk shake, chocolate, 74
    Mocha cream, 75
    Tea, mint, 117
    Tea, spiced, 118
    Tomato cooler, 118
Boiled salad dressing, 69
Braised chops, 98
Braised steak, 31, 98
Braised veal chops, 31
Breads, pastries and pastas:
    Bread cases, party, 75
    Croutons, 76
    Fried crumbs, 79
    Fritter batter, 78
    Garlic bread, 79
    Pastry, savory, 80
    Pastry, sweet, 68

Pizza pie, 80
Savory macaroni, 104
Spaghetti with
    meat sauce, 35
Buttermilk punch, 74

C

Cabbage salad, 49
Calorie-restricted diet:
    Menus, 119
    Principles of, 85
    Recipes, 93
    Substitutions, 89
Celery soup, 94
Cheese cake, 62
Chicken and orange, 40
Chicken and walnuts, 40
Chicken in the basket, 41
Chicken in wine, 101
Chicken riojana, 41
Chilled buttermilk
    soup, 94
Chilled tomato soup, 19
Chinese chicken
    soup, 20, 95
Chocolate cake, 53
Chocolate sauce pudding, 62
Christmas cake, 54
Christmas pudding, 63
Cinnamon crumble
    topping, 63
Coffee, iced, 75
Coleslaw, 106
Consommé, tomato, 95
Cooking measurements, 9
Cottage cheese:
    Dips, 76
    Nut balls, 77
    Potato salad, 50
Creamed chicken, 43
Creamed rice, 64
Creole vegetable soup, 20
Croutons, 76

Curried sauce, 114
Curried turkey, 43
Custard, vanilla, 64

D

Daily food quantities, 13
Desserts:
  Apple:
    Baked, 109
    Cake, 53
    Milk jelly, 109
    Roll, baked, 61
    Snow, jellied, 110
    Strudel, 59
  Banana, flambé, 61
  Banana, quick dessert, 67
  Cheese cake, 62
  Chocolate cake, 53
  Chocolate sauce pudding, 62
  Christmas cake, 54
  Cinnamon crumble
    topping, 63
  Custard, vanilla, 64
  Fruit nut loaf, 55
  Gingerbread, 55
  Ice cream, 65
  Introduction to, 60
  Junket, 66, 111
  Lemon meringue pie, 66
  Mocha sponge, 111
  Orange and pineapple
    delight, 112
  Orange and raisin slice, 56
  Orange biscuits, 56
  Orange cream, 112
  Pancakes, 67
  Pastry, sweet, 68
  Peaches, jellied, 110
  Pineapple dessert, 111
  Pineapple mint sherbet, 113
  Pudding, chocolate
    sauce, 62
  Pudding, Christmas, 63
  Rice, creamed, 64
  Scones, plain, 57

Devilled chicken, 102
Devilled walnuts, 77
Devil sauce, 102

F

Fad diets, 91
Filled milk, 74
Fillings, for rolls and
    sandwiches, 78
Fish:
  Baked, 22, 96
  Baked, marinated, 96
  Balls, 23
  Barbecue, 23
  Casserole, 24
  Chowder, 21
  Fillets:
    Psari plaki, 26
    Rolled, with anchovy
      sauce, 26
    Seasoned, 27
  Grilled, marinated, 25
  Grilled, with Italian
    dressing, 25
  Introduction to, 21
  Pie, with herbs, 24
  Poached, 25
  Salmon:
    And tomato savory, 97
    Snack, quick, 96
    Wizz, 26
  Soused, 97
  Tuna, sweet and sour, 27
French dressing, 70
French onion soup, 21
Fried crumbs, 79
Fried rice, 44
Fritter batter, 78
Fruit nut loaf, 55
Fruit salad, 110

G

Garlic bread, 79
Garlic spread, 70

Gingerbread, 55
Glazed carrots, 45
Green bean ring, 106
Green cabbage relish, 106
Grilled fish, Italian
    dressing, 25
Grilled marinated fish, 25

H

Hard sauce, 65
Hawaiian chicken, 103
Hawaiian rice, 44
Height-weight chart, 85

I

Ice cream, 65
Icing, warm, 60
Indian beef marinade, 99
Italian salad, 50

J

Jellied apple snow, 110
Jellied peaches, 110
Julienne soup, 95
Junket, 66, 111

L

Lemon filling, 54
Lemon meringue pie, 66
Lemon tingle, 117
Lenten vegetable pie, 79

M

Madras dry curry, 32
Malaysian lamb curry, 32
Marinated cucumbers, 51
Mashed potatoes, 46
Meats:
  Beef:
    In Burgundy, 30
    Marinade, Indian, 99
    Savory mince, 34

Steak, braised, 31, 98
Steak Diane, 100
Chicken:
  And orange, 40
  And walnuts, 40
  Creamed, 43
  Devilled, 102
  Hawaiian, 103
  In the basket, 31
  In wine, 107
  Riojana, 41
  Whole, braised with
    mushrooms, 44
Chops, braised, 98
Hawaiian rice, 44
Introduction to, 28
Madras dry curry, 32
Malaysian lamb curry, 32
Meat sauce, 99
Mexican rice, 33, 100
Spaghetti with meat
    sauce, 35
Turkey, curried, 43
Veal:
  And potato casserole, 38
  Chops, braised, 31
  Goulash, 36
  Marengo, 37, 101
  Ragout, 38
  Roast seasoned, 33
  Rolls, stuffed, 36
  Shredded, with celery, 34
Meat sauce, 99
Menus, calorie-restricted
    diet, 119
Menus, modified-fat diet, 82
Mexican rice, 33, 100
Mint sauce, 113
Mocha cream, 75
Mocha sponge, 111
Mock cream, 59
Modified-fat diet:
  Menus, 119
  Principles of, 11
  Recipes, 18
  Substitutions, 17

O

Orange and pineapple
    delight, 112
Orange and raisin slice, 56
Orange biscuits, 56
Orange cream, 112
Oven temperatures, 9

P

Pancakes, 67
Pastry (*see* Bread)
Pickled cucumbers, 107
Pickled onions, 107
Pickled red cabbage, 108
Pineapple and grapefruit
    salad, 108
Pineapple dessert, 111
Pineapple mint sherbet, 113
Piquant sauce, 71
Pizza pie, 80
Poached fish, 25
Polyunsaturated
    margarines, 13
Polyunsaturated
    mayonnaise, 13
Polyunsaturated oil, 12
Poultry (*see* Meat)
Psari plaki, 26
Pudding (*see* Dessert)

R

Raisin salad, 51
Rice riojana, 42
Rice salad, 51, 108
Riojana sauce, 42
Roast seasoned veal, 33
Rolled fish fillets,
    anchovy sauce, 26

S

Saffron rice, 46
Salads:
  Bean, 105
  Cabbage, 49

Coleslaw, 106
Cottage cheese potato, 50
Cucumbers, marinated, 50
Cucumbers, pickled, 107
Fruit, 110
Green bean ring, 105
Introduction to, 49
Italian, 50
Onions, pickled, 107
Pineapple and
    grapefruit, 108
Raisin, 51
Red cabbage, pickled, 108
Rice, 51, 108
Tomato, 109
Waldorf, 52
Yogurt potato, 52
Salmon and tomato savory, 97
Salmon snack, quick, 96
Salmon wizz, 26
Sauces, dressings,
    and relishes:
  Barbecue sauce, 69
  Boiled salad dressing, 69
  Cabbage relish, green, 106
  Curried sauce, 114
  Devil sauce, 102
  French dressing, 70
  Garlic spread, 70
  Hard sauce, 99
  Introduction to, 68
  Meat sauce, 65
  Mint sauce, 113
  Piquant sauce, 71
  Riojana sauce, 42
  Spiced dressing, 114
  Spiced vinegar for
    pickling, 114
  Tarragon dressing, 71
  Tartar sauce, 71
  Tomato chutney, 116
  Tomato dressing, 115
  Tomato sauce, 115
  White sauce, 72
  Yogurt salad dressing, 116
  Zero salad dressing, 117

Sautéed French beans, 46
Savory macaroni, 104
Savory mince, 34
Scalloped potatoes, 47
Scones, plain, 57
Seasoned fillets of fish, 27
Shredded veal and celery, 34
Soups:
  Asparagus, 94
  Buttermilk, chilled, 94
  Celery, 94
  Chinese chicken, 20, 95
  Cream, basic, 19
  Creole vegetable, 20
  Fish chowder, 21
  French onion, 21
  Introduction to, 18
  Julienne, 95
  Tomato, chilled, 19
  Tomato consommé, 95
Soused fish, 97
Spaghetti with meat sauce, 35
Spanish tart, 81
Spiced dressing, 114
Spiced tea, 118
Spiced vinegar for
  pickling, 114
Steak Diane, 100
Stuffed green peppers, 47
Stuffed tomatoes, 104
Stuffed veal rolls, 36
Sweet and sour tuna, 27

T

Tarragon dressing, 71
Tart, Spanish, 81
Tartar sauce, 71
Tomato and onion
  casserole, 105
Tomato chutney, 116
Tomato cooler, 118
Tomato dressing, 115
Tomato salad, 109
Tomato sauce, 115
Tomato scallop, 48
Tuna, sweet and sour, 27

V

Veal and potato
  casserole, 38
Veal goulash, 36
Veal marengo, 37, 101
Veal ragout, 38
Vegetables:
  Beans, sautéed French, 46
  Carrots, glazed, 45
  Green peppers, stuffed, 47
  Introduction to, 45
  Macaroni, savory, 104
  Onions, baked, 103
  Pie, Lenten vegetable, 79
  Potatoes, mashed, 46
  Potatoes, scalloped, 47
  Rice:
    Fried, 44
    Hawaiian, 44
    Mexican, 33, 100
    Riojana, 42
    Saffron, 46
  Sauté with tarragon
    dressing, 48
  Tomato and onion
    casserole, 105
  Tomato scallop, 48
  Tomatoes, stuffed, 104
Vienna mock cream, 59

W

Waldorf salad, 52
Walnut crescents, 58
Walnuts, devilled, 77
Weight reduction, 91
White sauce, 72
Whole chicken braised with
  mushrooms, 44

Y Z

Yogurt potato salad, 52
Yogurt salad dressing, 116
Zero salad dressing, 117